WAKE UP CHURCH

How to Be Ready
for the Return of Christ

Greg Wilburn

AMBASSADOR INTERNATIONAL
GREENVILLE, SOUTH CAROLINA & BELFAST, NORTHERN IRELAND

www.ambassador-international.com

With all of the confusing material available on preparing for the return of Christ, I am delighted to recommend this book. Clear, gospel-saturated, practical, and charged with convictional power, this book is a must read for all who seek to be faithful stewards in looking forward to the coming of Christ. Writing from the authority of Scripture and personal experience, Greg Wilburn challenges the church to wake up and take seriously the call that God has on each of our lives. I look forward with joy and expectation to see how God uses this work as a wake-up call for His people.

—CHAD LEWIS,
CAMPUS PASTOR
SOJOURN COMMUNITY CHURCH
LOUISVILLE, KENTUCKY

"There are many who call this Christian generation to be radical, but how? Many say its radical action . . . and I agree, but it's not action alone. A truly radical Christian life is first a mindset that comes from a deep understanding of radical Biblical truth. Greg Wilburn says that Christians' today are too focused on the here and now. That we have been seduced by the siren's call of living for heaven on earth rather than living as the bride of Christ anxiously awaiting our consummation in Christ's return. Read this book to regain a true counter cultural understanding of what it means to live a truly radical Biblical commitment and help wake up the church."

—J. MACK STILES
DUBAI, UAE
AUTHOR OF *MARKS OF A MESSENGER*

Wake Up Church
HOW TO BE READY FOR THE RETURN OF CHRIST

© 2010 Greg Wilburn

All rights reserved

Printed in the United States of America

ISBN: 978-1-935507-34-5

Cover Design & Page Layout by David Siglin of A&E Media

AMBASSADOR INTERNATIONAL
Emerald House
427 Wade Hampton Blvd.
Greenville, SC 29609, USA
www.ambassador-international.com

AMBASSADOR BOOKS
The Mount
2 Woodstock Link
Belfast, BT6 8DD, Northern Ireland, UK
www.ambassador-international.com

The colophon is a trademark of Ambassador

Table of Contents

A Wake-Up Call

What is this life all about? Why do you breathe? Why do you wake up in the morning? Why are you even on this earth?

We are here to prepare for an eternity of joyfully giving glory to the eternal God. But instead, we live our lives as though this life were it. We live our lives as though the current state of this world is our home. We cling to people, places and things as though these are what we were ultimately made for. We become fixated and attached to the petty things of this life as though our ultimate satisfaction and hope were in those things.

Have you forgotten what you were made for, Christian? Have you forgotten what you should be longing for, the appearing of the glory of our great God and Savior Jesus Christ? Our taste buds for heaven have been dulled by the bitter deceitful desires of this world. Our hearts have grown cold to the warmth of the Father's heavenly love. Our eyes of faith have been shut to the realm of God's eternal beauty, but our eyes of flesh are wide open to the allurements of what we see here and now. Our minds have shrunk to perceive only the vain and shallow and are now incapable of perceiving the depths of the Holy One.

This is a wake-up call, church. The dawn of glory is on the horizon. Our crucified and risen Lord says, "Surely I am coming

soon" (Rev. 22:20). Paul writes, "...the hour has come for you
to wake from sleep. For salvation is nearer to us now than when
we first believed. The night is far gone; the day is at hand" (Rom.
13:11-12). Each day that passes is a step closer to the bright
and glorious appearing of our Lord Jesus. And yet each day our
minds sit in darkness to this reality. We rarely think of the weight
of this truth, that one day very soon we will see our King face to
face. And because we do not think of it, we do not anticipate it
or live in light of it. Therefore, we are not ready!

One of Satan's greatest attacks on the church is to cause her
to forget her future destination. For most people, not knowing
where they are going in life can lead to a sense of apathy, complacency, confusion and despair. The same is true for us as Christians.
We must not forget where we are headed and what awaits us. The
church must develop a stronger vision for eternity. If there is one
thing I see lacking in many fellow Christians, it is this lack of excitement and anticipation for the coming of Christ.

We must fight to keep this anticipation before us so that we
will be ready when He comes. The culture we live in teaches us
to focus on the opposite—the here and the now. Our secular society instructs us that there is no life beyond this life. What you
see is what you get. There is nothing more to hope for. Live for
today! Our materialistic culture tells us to put our hope in possessions, but we know that we have "a better possession and an
abiding one" (Heb. 10:34).

For many years, Americans have trusted in the great wealth
and abundance of our country but now, with the uncertainties
of our economy, people are not resting so securely. What is
certain is that this country, along with all other countries, will
eventually collapse under God's judgment. In that day, God's
people will be ushered into "a better country, that is, a heavenly

one" (Heb. 11:16) where the Lord Jesus will reign as King forever. Those who have not entered into His kingdom by faith will be left to eternal damnation.

The truth is, the more we anticipate and long for the coming of Christ the more radically we will live the Christian life here and now. Yet, sadly, there are some teachers among the church in our day and time who are saying the opposite. These influences within the church tend to deemphasize the life hereafter and exalt the life of the here and now. Whether trying to gain prosperity in this life (the prosperity gospel) or create a utopian society (the newly packaged social gospel of the postmoderns[1]), these people are straying from the biblical view concerning the hope of the gospel and future judgment. Due to the postmodern ethos of our culture, many within the church are saying that "life is about the journey, not the destination. It's about the search, not the arrival."

There is much emphasis on how the kingdom of God is present now. This is true. The kingdom has come, but we must realize that there is much more to come. There is a destination, arrival and consummation we must look forward to. As Christians we are "sojourners and exiles" (1 Pet. 2:11) who confess with the Apostle Paul that "to live is Christ and to die is gain" (Phil. 1:21). If we do not begin to have this attitude, we will not be ready when He appears. In the rest of this book, we will look at what it means to prepare for His coming.

---

1 The social gospel, a product of 19th century to early 20th century modern liberal theology, is the belief that the ultimate message and good news of the Bible has *nothing* to do with salvation from sin and God's eternal judgment but everything to do with deliverance in the present from poverty and injustice. This worldview has been newly packaged in the most recent cultural shift called "postmodernism."

Chapter I

Longing for His Appearing

The Bride Anticipates the Groom

As human beings, we are all wired with similar needs and longings. In spite of our differences and diversity of appearance, culture, personality, beliefs, values and understanding, we all have some very deep-rooted similarities. To survive, all human beings have basic needs such as food and water. Not only do all people have physical needs, but we have emotional, mental and spiritual needs as well. Every person has a need for intimacy and a desire to be loved, from the newborn baby, to the rebellious teen, to the burnt-out middle-aged man, to the dying elderly woman. We all have a need for love.

Along with this need for love, ultimately all human beings have a desire to be happy and satisfied. Blaise Pascal makes this same observation by stating, "All men seek happiness. This is without exception. Whatever different means they employ, they all tend to this end. The cause of some going to war and of others avoiding it is the same desire in both, attended with different views. The will never takes the least step but to this object. This is the motive of every action of every man, even of those who hang themselves."[2]

2 Blaise Pascal, Pascal's Pensees, trans. W.F. Trotter (New York: E.P. Dutton, 1958) 1.13, thought #425

Because of mankind's desire to be happy, death is something to be feared by all. To have happiness, you must have life. At death life ends; therefore, the possibility of happiness ends. All people have a longing to live forever and to live happily forever. This is because God "has put eternity into man's heart" (Eccl. 3:11).

Deep inside, all human beings also have an innate sense of right and wrong. Though many times distorted and suppressed, all people have a built-in sense of morality (Rom. 2:14-15). Along with this is a built-in sense that there is such a thing as truth and falsehood. And the truth that is clearly revealed to all men is that there is a God, though many suppress this truth (Rom. 1:18-20). All of the desires that mankind has—love, joy, permanence, and truth—are wrapped up in and flow from God. All of mankind has these longings because they point us to our need for God, to know Him and love Him. We were made to worship and enjoy the true God. Man's longing is meant to be fulfilled in Him.

An Analogy of Longing

One of the greatest expressions of human longing and anticipation can be found in a man and woman who are awaiting the consummation of marriage. Prior to marriage, they have committed themselves to each other and await the future fulfillment of that commitment that will take place on their wedding day. In many cases, the couple has been spending much time getting to know each other and growing in their feelings for one another. Their excitement and anticipation begins to build as they get closer and closer to the day when they will be intimately united as one, enjoying the full and unhindered expression of love for one another. A good friend described his feelings leading up to his marriage: "It was an extreme longing, a stomach-churning longing, a can't-wait-to-be-with-each-other kind of thing."

Reflecting on her feelings during this time, his wife said, "In my longing at one point I thought to myself, 'Is it ever going to happen? Will there ever be a consummation?' I longed for more. I longed for the day there would be no restrictions and no distance. I longed for the day our lives would be completely intertwined." In these expressions, we see just how intense this longing for the marriage consummation can be.

Longing For a Greater Marriage

Though this longing and anticipation for the consummation of marriage is intense, there is an even greater marriage to long for and anticipate. In fact, our longing and anticipation for this greater marriage should be incomparably stronger. The earthly marriage between a man and a woman, though good and special, is symbolic of the greater marriage. It is but a dim reflection of the more superior marriage. If the symbol is so precious and beautiful, how much more is the object it points to?

What is this object that the marriage of a man and woman symbolizes? What is this greater marriage that we speak of? Paul explains this for us in Ephesians 5:22-27 and 31-32:

"Wives, submit to your own husbands, as to the Lord. For the husband is the head of the wife even as Christ is the head of the church, his body, and is himself its Savior. Now as the church submits to Christ, so also wives should submit in everything to their husbands. Husbands, love your wives, as Christ loved the church and gave himself up for her, that he might sanctify her, having cleansed her by the washing of water with the word, so that he might present the church to himself in splendor, without spot or wrinkle or any such thing, that she might be holy and without blemish. ... 'Therefore a man shall leave his father and mother and hold fast to his wife, and the two shall become one flesh.' This mystery is profound, and I am saying that it refers to Christ and the church."

Here we see Paul giving instructions to husbands and wives concerning their roles in the marriage relationship. This marriage relationship and its roles are rooted in Christ's relationship to the church. The wife is to submit to her husband as the church submits to Christ and his leadership (v. 22-24). The husband is to sacrificially love his wife as Christ loved the church and died for her (v. 25). The husband is to lead and nourish his wife just as Christ leads and nourishes the church through his word (v. 26-29). In verse 32, Paul states very clearly that this marriage relationship between a man and a woman points to Christ and the church. This relationship is a symbolic picture of Christ's relationship to the church. This joyful submission and trust, this sacrificial love and servant leadership found in the marriage relationship, is a beautifully symbolic picture of the even greater union between Christ and His Bride, the church.

Paul, speaking of this symbolic marriage between a man and woman, quotes Genesis 2:24 and states, "Therefore a man shall leave his father and mother and hold fast to his wife, and the two shall become one flesh" (Eph. 5:31). In this statement, we see an expression of deep and mysterious intimacy as the man and woman come together in sexual union within the marriage context, thus becoming one flesh. The intimate, interconnectedness of this one flesh union is so amazing that Paul must confess in verse 32, "This mystery is profound, and I am saying that it refers to Christ and the church." This intimate, one-flesh union between husband and wife mysteriously points to the even greater and more satisfying union between Christ and the church. This deeply enriching physical and temporary union between man and woman, points to the infinitely more enriching spiritual and eternal union between Christ and His people.

The Blessedness of Being United to Christ

At this point we need to ask ourselves the question: What is it that makes this union with Christ so special and satisfying?

How does union with Christ far exceed the blessedness of a man and woman being united in marriage? What does it mean to be united to Christ?

So far we have acknowledged that there is a special beauty, joy, and intimacy in the husband and wife relationship. Though this is true, men and women who are single can still live happy and meaningful lives. Marriage is not essential for the happiness and meaning of one's existence, though for some this may seem the case. Yet, union to Christ is essential. We as human beings cannot find ultimate satisfaction and meaning without being intimately united in a relationship to the Son of God, Jesus Christ.

Ever since the rebellion and fall of mankind, man has been separated from God at birth. In the book of Exodus, we see God in His mercy pursuing His people with redemptive love and supernaturally rescuing them from slavery in Egypt. He then gave them His holy law (the 10 commandments as well as many other laws) to be perfectly followed and obeyed. God is holy and therefore requires absolute perfect obedience to His law in order for us to live. Mankind could not then and cannot now perfectly obey God's law. Man is bound to the requirements of God's law, yet is unable to fulfill them. In essence, man is married to God's law. Just as a husband and wife are bound to each other in marriage, mankind is bound and married to God's law. And this is not a good and happy marriage.

After Paul expresses the binding nature of the law, by using marriage as an analogy in Romans 7:1-3, he states in verse 5, "For while we were living in the flesh, our sinful passions, aroused by the law, were at work in our members to bear fruit for death." Separated from Christ man is united to another spouse, the law, which aroused sinful passions within us resulting in us bearing fruit for death. Though "the law is holy, and the commandment is holy and righteous and good" (Rom 7:12), "…sin, seizing an opportunity through the commandment, deceived me and through it killed me" (Rom. 7:11). In other words, when we are told not to do something, it makes us want to do it even more because of our corrupt nature. The outcome of being bound to the law of God is to be further bound to sin and the outcome of being bound to sin, ultimately, is being bound to death (Rom. 6:23).

Man in his natural state, is married (united and bound) to God's law, sin, and death. We are under the curse of eternal condemnation and judgment because of our failure to obey God's law. Because of our deep-rooted sinful nature, the law is powerless to change or save us. But praise God that He "has done what the law, weakened by the flesh, could not do. By sending His own Son in the likeness of sinful flesh and for sin, he condemned sin in the flesh, in order that the righteous requirement of the law might be fulfilled in us" (Rom. 8:3-4). We could not be saved by following God's law because of our depraved nature. Therefore, God sent His Son, Jesus, to this earth to perfectly obey His law for us and die the death we deserved, so that we could stand righteous before God. Through faith in Christ we have now been "released from the law" (Rom. 7:6) and have "died to the law…so that [we] may belong to another" (v. 4). Because of this "there is therefore now no condemnation for those who are in Christ Jesus" (Rom. 8:1). Through faith in Christ, we are freed from the condemnation of God. We are freed from our marriage bond to sin and death and are alive with and united to Christ Jesus.

Being united to Christ means we are now a new people who have new life. We are now "a new creation.…The old has passed away; behold, the new has come" (2 Cor. 5:17). Like a caterpillar transformed into a butterfly, we have a new way of moving and living. To be united to Christ means to be united with him in his death and resurrection. We see this in Romans 6:4: "We were buried therefore with him by baptism into death, in order that, just as Christ was raised from the dead by the glory of the Father, we too might walk in newness of life."

When we repent of our rebellion against God and put our trust in Jesus, we are immediately ushered into this mysterious union with Christ's death and resurrection. This means that we have died to our former sinful way of life and are now alive to the ways of God. Baptism means "to be immersed." At conversion, we were spiritually immersed into the death and burial of Christ. Our old sinful way of life was buried with Christ, and as Christ was raised from the dead, we now have risen to walk in newness of life.

In light of this union with Christ, Paul tells us in Colossians 3:1-3, "If then you have been raised with Christ, seek the things that are above, where Christ is, seated at the right hand of God. Set your minds on things that are above, not on things that are on earth. For you have died, and your life is hidden with Christ in God." We have died to our old sinful self, have the new resurrection life of Jesus inside of us, and are now called to live in that reality. Our spiritual union with Jesus has given us a blessed new life, and we are now called to live in that new life. To be united to Christ and to share in His death and resurrection means to set our minds on things above, where Christ is, and to turn our minds away from the sinful ways of this world.

Not only does union with Christ mean freedom from the bondage and condemnation of the law and liberation from the power of sin, but it also means being immersed into an intimate love relationship with the Savior, whose source of endless love comes from our great Father. Jesus says in John 15:9, "As the Father has loved me, so have I loved you. Abide in my love." As a husband and wife intimately abide in each other's love, we, the Bride of

Christ, are to intimately abide in His love. Jesus tells us how to do that in verse 10, "If you keep my commandments, you will abide in my love." Out of the overflow of trusting in the saving love of Jesus displayed at the cross, we seek to obey His commandments. And His commandments are these: Love God with all your heart, mind, soul, and strength; and love your neighbor as yourself.

Being united to Christ thus means that we now have this new love relationship with God as our Father and Jesus as our Spouse, whom we are to lovingly submit to and obey. We were created to know and love God. We were created to worship Him with all of our being and to enjoy His love forever. Because of our sin we were once alienated from this glorious reality, but since our precious Bridegroom loved us and gave himself up for us (Gal. 2:20), by faith in Him we are now forgiven and eternally secure in the satisfying love of God. As the Bride of Christ, we are now called to embrace His love and pour it back to Him. We are to love Him with all of our desires, thoughts, and actions. We are to trust Him, cherish Him above all, and live our whole lives for His glory and praise. We are to daily grow deeper in intimacy with Him through talking to Him in prayer. We are to extend God's great love to our fellow man and to point them to the grace found in Jesus Christ.

This new life of abiding in Christ's love leads to true everlasting joy. That's why Jesus continues into John 15:11 saying, "These things I have spoken to you, that my joy may be in you, and that your joy may be full." To abide in the love of Christ is to abide in the joy of Christ, and Christ's joy is fullness of joy. Christ is not lacking in joy and happiness, and He calls us to walk into His joy by walking in His love, through trusting Him and obeying His commandments.

Living and dwelling in God's great love revealed in the death and resurrection of Jesus for sinners is what it means to be united to Jesus. Worshiping and rejoicing in God for His greatness and goodness and joyfully obeying His commands is what it means to share in intimate union with Jesus. And, ultimately, to be united to Jesus means to set our minds with great anticipation upon the coming consummation of this glorious and eternally enriching marriage union.

The Future Marriage Consummation

We were once dead in sin (Eph. 2:1) and headed for eternal hell separated from God because of our disobedience, but through faith in Christ our Savior, we now have a new destination to look forward to. At conversion, we became united to Christ and therefore, dead to sin and alive to God as new creatures. But our union with Christ is not final as it now stands. There is a future consummation that is to come. Romans 6:5 states, "For if we have been united with him in a death like his, we shall certainly be united with him in a resurrection like his." There is a future resurrection of our bodies that we wait for. Colossians 3:4 states, "When Christ who is your life appears, then you also will appear with him in glory." Christ first came to accomplish the work of redemption for God's people, but when He comes again He will restore His people fully to himself and take them into His glory. We as Christians are justified sinners (sinners declared righteous) who have been adopted by the Father, united to Christ, and indwelt with the Holy Spirit. We have already received so much grace and blessing by God, and yet we still struggle with sin on a daily basis. Our natures are still corrupted by indwelling sin and our bodies are subject to suffering and decay. The world we live in is full of brokenness and evil. We await and long for things to be made right. We await our final and glorious marriage consummation with the Son of God, who will usher us into the glorious presence of the Father.

Now we as Christians are united to Christ and share in His love and holiness, but one day we will fully share in His love and holiness without the hindrance of sin (1 John 3:2). We have begun to experience this blessed reality, but there is much more to come, just as a man and woman engaged to be married have tasted sweet fellowship and yet have much more in store at the consummation of marriage. As Christians, in this life, we have tasted the sweetness of being united to our blessed Savior, but the consummation of that sweet fellowship comes at the end of the age. This idea is expressed by the Puritan, Thomas Watson:

> "In this life there is only the contract. The Jews had a time set between their engagement and marriage, sometimes a year or more. In this life there is only the engagement and contract; promises are made on both sides, and love passes secretly between Christ and the soul. He gives some smiles of his face, and the soul sends up her sighs and drops tears of love. But all this is only preliminary work, and something leading up to the marriage. The glorious completing and solemnizing of the marriage is reserved for heaven. There is the marriage supper of the Lamb (Rev. 19:9) and the bed of glory perfumed with love where the souls of the elect shall be perpetually consoling themselves."[3]

In Revelation 19:6-9, we see this consummation of our marriage to Christ. "Then I heard what seemed to be the voice of a great multitude, like the roar of many waters and like the sound of mighty peals of thunder, crying out, 'Hallelujah! For the Lord

---

3 Thomas Watson, *A Godly Man's Picture* (Edinburgh, UK: The Banner of Truth Trust, 2007), 242.

God the Almighty reigns. Let us rejoice and exult and give him the glory, for the marriage of the Lamb has come, and his Bride has made herself ready; it was granted her to clothe herself with fine linen, bright and pure'—for the fine linen is the righteous deeds of the saints. And the angel said to me, 'Write this: Blessed are those who are invited to the marriage supper of the Lamb.'"

After the outpouring of God's judgment at the end of the age, we see a great multitude from heaven roar with praise to God because the marriage supper of the Lamb has come. Heaven bursts out with rejoicing and celebration because the final consummation of Christ's marriage to the church has come. At this point there will be no more distance and separation. There will be no more hindrances and barriers to intimacy. Sin will be banished. Struggles will have ceased. We will be fully united spiritually to Jesus Christ, our Lord and Savior, our Friend and Lover. In our glorified and resurrected bodies we will stand before our precious Bridegroom, beholding His glory, drenched in fullness of joy! Soaked in His love, our hearts will pound with inexpressible gladness and our tongues will shout with uncontrollable rejoicing! We will party! We will feast! We will begin the eternal honeymoon and unending celebration! This is what we as Christians have to look forward to.

Earlier I shared my friend and his wife's reflections on their feelings of anticipation leading up to their marriage. In describing his wedding day, my friend said, "Everything culminated on the wedding day and there is no other word to describe it but 'celebration.' When Kirstin walked down the aisle it was a moment of transcendence. Everything was building up to this moment in time."

This is true of our relationship with Jesus Christ. Everything will culminate on the great wedding day when He returns and there will be no other word but 'celebration.' It will be a transcendent moment that will last forever. Everything is building up to that moment, when we as Christ's Bride will be raised to life and will meet our perfect Lover face to face. We will look into the eyes of the one who died to rescue us from the clutches of eternal death, in order that we would be brought to this day standing before Him and the Father, filled with perfect and never-ending joy.

Do You Long for this Great Day?

Words cannot express the great joy we will experience as we are finally fully united to our Savior and brought into the fullness of the Father's love. Words cannot capture the beauty we will see as we look upon our precious Lord. Words cannot come close to articulating this glorious day of our marriage with the Lamb. Looking forward to this great day, Jesus was provoked to earnestly prayer to the Father in John 17:24: "Father, I desire that they also, whom you have given me, may be with me where I am, to see my glory that you have given me because you loved me before the foundation of the world." Jesus passionately desires that His Bride be with him. He longs for His people to be with Him and to see His glory. Christ's glory is wrapped up in the Father's eternal love bestowed upon Him, and He wants us to come to Him and behold this glorious love forever. Jesus truly longs for you to be with Him. Do you believe that? If you are united to Christ (a part of those the Father has given Him), then the amazing truth is, that the mighty King Jesus earnestly longs for you personally to be with Him. If you are not a child of the Father and united to Jesus, by turning from your sin and trusting in Christ you can be.

It truly is an amazing reality that the Son of God who has all authority and power passionately longs for sinners like you and me to be with Him in glory. Such is the amazing grace of our God! If our Savior longs for us to be with Him in glory, shouldn't we also long to be with Him in glory? This should be the reality for every person who is a true child of God. We see this very clearly in the New Testament. Hebrews 9:28 states that "Christ, having been offered once to bear the sins of many, will appear a second time, not to deal with sin but to save those who are eagerly waiting for him." Christ died for the sins of many at His first coming. When He comes back, those He died to save will be ushered into the fullness of the salvation He died to accomplish. They will escape the wrath of God and be brought into eternal glory. From the text, we see that those who are eagerly waiting for Him will be saved. What does this mean? Are we saved by something we do? No. But our eager anticipation for His coming will be a sign or evidence that we truly know Him, and our total lack of eager anticipation will be evidence that we don't truly know Him. This is a serious thing.

What about you? Do you eagerly wait for the coming of Christ? Test yourself. This should be the reality for every true Christian. Titus 2:13 says that the children of God are the ones who are "waiting for our blessed hope, the appearing of the glory of our great God and Savior Jesus Christ." Phil. 3:20 states, "But our citizenship is in heaven, and from it we await a Savior, the Lord Jesus Christ."

In fact, this longing and anticipation for Christ's coming is described in quite intense language. Rom. 8:22–23 states, "For we know that the whole creation has been groaning together in the pains of childbirth until now. And not only the creation, but we ourselves, who have the firstfruits of the Spirit, groan inwardly as we wait eagerly for adoption as sons, the redemption of our bodies." Since the fall of mankind, all of creation has been groaning and desperately longing for fullness of redemption and renewal. Our world is gripped with the curse of sin, decay, and death, and it groans like a woman giving birth to a child for the lifting of this dreadful curse. All of creation aches for the return of Jesus and for the establishment of the new heavens and the new earth where righteousness will dwell. Yet not only does the creation long for this coming day of redemption; we as Christians "groan inwardly as we wait eagerly for adoption as sons, the redemption of our bodies" (v. 23). Those who truly know Christ and have tasted the sweetness of His grace know that there is nothing better in all the universe. That is why we want more of it. We want to go deeper in His love and experience the infinite fullness of this supremely satisfying grace. Therefore, we groan inwardly and wait eagerly for the day when Christ returns and gives us resurrected glorified bodies that are able to take in the eternal overwhelming pleasure of God's fatherly love. As Christians, our hearts should burn with desire for this great day of redemption. Our souls should ache and hunger for our coming King. Our minds should be filled with thoughts of eager anticipation for His glorious appearing.

Why We Don't Long for Christ's Coming

At this point you might be saying to yourself, "I don't have this sort of longing for Christ's return. How can I?"

First, we must realize that a growing longing for Christ's return only comes by God's grace through the work of His Holy Spirit in our hearts. The Holy Spirit must give us eyes to see and hearts to feel the greatness of this coming reality. Second, though this is true, God gives us means to act upon that the Holy Spirit uses to bring about this reality in our hearts and lives.

One vital thing we must do is examine ourselves. We must examine our hearts and see what it is we value and treasure the most. What we treasure most will be identified by what we take the greatest delight in. That which you enjoy most, you will love most. Your greatest love will be your greatest joy. Jesus put it this way, "For where your treasure is, there your heart will be also" (Matt.

6:21). Whatever you consider to be of greatest value will be what your heart loves most. And our words and actions will be indicators of what we treasure most. "For out of the abundance of the heart the mouth speaks" (Matt. 12:34b). Our words reflect what is in our hearts. Whatever is the joyful and constant topic on your tongue, whether sports, music, family, sex, money, career, or politics, this will be the indicator of what you love and cherish most in your heart. And the reason we treasure and love certain things above others is because we see them as giving us the greatest pleasure or joy.

The problem with this is that our differing perceptions of what will bring us the greatest joy are not consistent with reality. The reality is that we were made for the glory of God (Isa. 43:7, Rom. 11:36) and He is the only one who truly satisfies (Isa. 55:1-3, Jer. 2:13). But instead of worshiping Him and enjoying Him, we have exchanged His glory and truth and have worshipped and treasured created things (Rom. 1:22-25). The reason for this is that in our sinful state we are deceived to believe that created things are better than the Creator. That is why the Bible describes sin as "deceitful desires" (Ephesians 4:22). The idols and worldly treasures of our hearts do not offer the life and joy they claim to give. Not only are we deceived into believing lies about our earthly treasures, but we are also many times, even as Christians, blind to the supremely satisfying beauty that is found in God, displayed through Jesus Christ. Being blind to the glory of God is the reason we do not long for the return of Jesus as we should. We walk through life with our eyes of faith shut to the captivating glory of Christ but open to the things of this world. We are more pleased by entertainment than the infinite God. In essence, we have a small view of God and His glory revealed in Christ, and we have a larger view of infinitely lesser things, such as people, places, and things. We do not treasure Christ above all else because we do not see Him as better than all else. We do not treasure Christ above all else because we do not see Him for the supremely valuable Person He really is and for the supremely loving act He has done for us at the cross. Because we do not see Christ as He really is, we do not desperately long for His return as we should.

In order to grow in our longing for the return of Jesus, we must grow in our understanding of the greatness of God which is revealed in our Savior. We must come to the realization that "He is the radiance of the glory of God and the exact imprint of his nature" (Heb. 1:3). All that God the Father is can be found in Jesus Christ. Jesus Christ is the perfect display of the excellence of God. The limitless power and rule of God, the unsearchable wisdom and knowledge of God, the spotless purity of God, the incomprehensible holiness of God, the flawless justice of God, the unshakeable truth of God, the never-ending love of God, the unfathomable grace of God, the unsurpassable faithfulness of God, the incomparable beauty of God and the unchanging perfection of God are perfectly summed up and revealed in Jesus Christ, the Son of God. This is the great Savior and Person that we are to long for. None can compare with Him.

What it all comes down to is that we must come to the same realization that David did in Ps. 63:3, "Because your steadfast love is better than life, my lips will praise you." God, who is love, is better than life itself. The eternal God of perfect love is full of infinitely greater worth then anything and everything you could ever experience or encounter in this universe. Your greatest worldly treasures, your greatest earthly joys, your most pleasurable experiences in this life, cannot even come close in comparison to the supremely satisfying God over all. His steadfast love truly is better than life. And the manifestation of His steadfast love has been expressed in such a mysteriously beautiful way that no greater definition or expression of love could ever be given. In a prayer in his book, *Don't Waste Your Life*, John Piper points us to this supreme love: "Father, love is this: At great expense you made yourself my glory and my boast. The cost was infinite by which you made yourself the Treasure of my life. You sent your Son, the blazing center of your beauty and your love. You gave him up to mockery, betrayal, thorns, the whip, the rod, the fists, the nails, the shame, and death. For what? To swallow up your wrath, and satisfy your righteousness, and bury all my sins as far as east is from the west and in the deepest sea, so that I might come home and see the galaxy. This is your love, O God, not to make much of me, but do whatever must be done so that I waken to the joy of making much of you through all eternity."[4]

God's steadfast love is better than life. At the cross of the precious Son of God, this supreme love was displayed and poured out for us to know and enjoy forever. We truly do have a great God and a perfect Savior. Is He your greatest love? Is He your greatest treasure? We must examine our hearts and repent of our idolatry and devaluing of God. We must seek His Word and cry out for the Holy Spirit to give us spiritual eyes to see His supreme worth. Only then will we truly long for the return of Jesus. The more we understand His greatness and taste its sweetness in our hearts, the more we will desperately long for His return.

The Reason for this Book

The whole reason I write this book is so that the church would be prepared for the return of Jesus. In my opinion, the evangelical church as a whole has not given the due attention

---

4 John Piper, *Don't Waste Your Life* (Wheaton, IL: Crossway Books, 2003), 186. Used by permission of Crossway, a publishing ministry of Good News Publishers, Wheaton, IL 60187, www.crossway.org.

and proper focus to the Second Coming of Jesus that I believe is clearly warranted from the emphasis put upon it in Scripture. How will we be ready for His return if we have not adjusted our lens to a right biblical focus concerning this matter? We cannot be prepared for the coming of Jesus, if we do not long for His coming and live in expectation of it. We cannot long for His appearing unless we grow in our understanding of the greatness and goodness of our God and Savior who is to come. It is true, we do not know the day or the hour of Jesus' Second Coming, but Scripture says we will know the times and the seasons (Matt. 24:33, 36; 1 Thess. 5:1). The Bible tells us to be watchful and ready for His return. We as believers should not be taken by surprise. His coming will take nonbelievers by surprise. To them He will come like a thief in the night (1 Thess. 5:2-3). First Thessalonians 5:4 states, "But you are not in darkness, brothers, for that day to surprise you like a thief."

My fear is that many professing Christians will be taken by surprise because they will be focused simply on this life and the things of this world, having no regard or longing for the things of eternity. May God use this book to prepare the Bride of Christ for the return of their beloved Bridegroom and King. In the following chapters, we will look at specific exhortations that Scripture gives us in order to prepare for His coming.

CHAPTER 2

Love the Truth

As we begin to think about the return of Jesus and what it means to be ready for His coming, we must examine the times we live in and the great need we have in this hour of history. We live in a day and age where truth and morality are relative. Universal morality and absolute truth are seen as intolerant beliefs that are out of step with our ever-changing world. The air we breathe in the West is the air of postmodernism which tells us that there is no overarching truth or meaning in the universe, and therefore we must make our own truth and meaning. This message can be found anywhere from the media to the universities, from the arts to the sciences, from politics to religion.

Due to our increasingly multicultural society, our culture has become a melting pot of religious views. This has led to an increase in pluralistic tendencies. Pluralism is the belief that all religions are seen as equally valid and true. No one religion is considered better than any other. It is seen as politically incorrect and offensive in our society to say that one religion is the right religion.

This postmodern air of Western culture has not just been contained in the non-Christian world but has also spread like a virus into the church. According to George Barna's statistics, only 32% of so called born-again believers actually believe in absolute truth. Christianity, which is based upon absolute truth claims, has become deeply infected by the prevailing worldview

of our postmodern culture. David Wells makes this same observation of the Western church's disregard for truth: "…when
we listen to the church today, at least in the West, we are often
left with the impression that Christianity actually has very little
to do with truth. Christianity is only about feeling better about
ourselves, about leaping over our difficulties, about being more
satisfied, about having better relationships, about getting along
with our mothers-in-law, about understanding teenage rebellion,
about coping with our unreasonable bosses, about finding greater
sexual satisfaction, about getting rich, about receiving our own
private miracles and much else besides. It is about everything except truth."[5] This is indeed the disturbing reality we find in the
Western church. We have conformed to the spirit of our age and
loosened our confidence in the truth.

When we look at biblical and historic Christianity, we couldn't
find a more radically different reality. Wells, commenting on the
apostles' proclamation of the gospel writes:

> "This proclamation was not simply a telling of their pri-
> vate experience, nor just their own personal opinion. It
> was not what had become truth for *them*. It was a procla-
> mation about truth for *all*. The gospel, which is the same
> gospel for all people, in all ages, and at all times, is 'the
> word of truth' (Eph. 1:13; see also Col. 1:5; 2 Thess. 2:13;
> Heb. 10:26). Faith is about 'obeying the truth' (Gal. 5:7; 1
> Pet. 1:22). Those who are condemned are condemned be-
> cause they do not believe 'the truth' (2 Thess. 2:12). Those
> who are depraved in mind are depraved because they are
> 'deprived of the truth' (1 Tim. 6:5). This faith, which is

---

5 David Wells, The Courage to Be Protestant: Truth-Lovers, Marketers, and Emergents in the Postmodern World (Grand Rapids, MI: Wm. B. Eerdmans Publishing Co.,
2008), 88.

all about the truth that God has given us, is delivered through his truth (2 Cor. 4:2) and is made effective by the Spirit who is the Spirit of truth (1 John 5:6). Christianity, in short, is from first to last all about *truth*! It is about he who is the Way, the *Truth*, and the Life."[6]

To be a Christian means to have your life centered on truth.

As Christians, we are to center our lives upon truth, because the God we worship and love is the God who is truth. "Truth in the Bible" writes J. I. Packer, "is a quality of persons primarily, and of propositions only secondarily: it means stability, reliability, firmness, trustworthiness, the quality of a person who is entirely self-consistent, sincere, realistic, and undeceived. God is such a person: truth, in this sense, is His nature, and He has not got in Him to be anything else. That is why He cannot lie (Titus 1:2; cf. Num. 23:19; 1 Sam. 15:29; Heb. 6:18). That is why His words to us are true, and cannot be other than true. They are the index of reality: they show us things as they really are and as they will be for us in the future according to whether we heed God's words to us or not."[7]

God is truth; therefore all that He communicates is truth. God in His complete trustworthiness has overflowed in perfect and true communication to mankind. He has given us His true words, which are found in the Bible. God Himself has spoken and His "word is truth" (John 17:17). Without His Word, without His true communication, we would not know Him. Without the Bible, we would not be able to have a relationship with the most glorious being in the universe, namely, God Himself. Relationships are built on knowledge. Without true knowledge of a person, you cannot have a real and authentic relationship with that person. No knowledge or inaccurate knowledge of a person will

---

6 Ibid, 76.
7 J.I. Packer, Knowing God (Intervarsity Press, 1973), 102.

lead to a fabricated relationship with that person. God's Word is truth and it is through His trustworthy Word that we come to truly know Him.

God's words are not mere words for the sake of words. God's Word leads us to a Person. The Bible ultimately leads us to the Person of Jesus Christ, who is the one who leads us to the all-satisfying God. In John 14:6, Jesus says, "I am the way, and the truth, and the life. No one comes to the Father except through me." The Bible points us to Jesus, the Son of God, because Jesus is the way to the Father. Jesus is the truth, the perfect revelation of God the Father, who is truth. Jesus is the life that leads mankind to true life in God. As Christians, we must care deeply about truth, because we worship the God of truth who has given us His Word of truth, which points us to true life found in His perfect Son, who is the Truth.

Enemy of the Truth and Mankind's Slavery to his Lies

Down through the centuries, there have been many wars. The countless wars in this world's history have been fought for countless different reasons. But one reason that wars are sometimes fought is for the freedom of one's country and the preservation of the lives of its citizens. For freedom and life to be gained, the enemy must be identified and defeated.

From the beginning of human history until now, mankind has been caught in a spiritual war between the kingdom of truth and the kingdom of lies. God is truth and He created human beings to know, experience, and live in the truth of His love. Yet we learn from Scripture that there is an enemy of the truth who has swayed the hearts of every man into the bondage of his lies and away from the truth of God.

This enemy of the truth is the devil, whom Jesus says "was a murderer from the beginning, and has nothing to do with the truth, because there is no truth in him. When he lies, he speaks out of his own character, for he is a liar and the father of lies" (John 8:44). Satan is the enemy of God and therefore the enemy of truth. All that God is—trustworthy, stable and reliable—the devil is not. There is no truth in the devil. He is a liar who is out "to steal and kill and destroy" (John 10:10). The devil, who is a liar, deceived mankind who was created in the likeness of God, and convinced them to rebel against God (Gen. 3:1-5). Adam and Eve bought the lie and plunged the rest of mankind into slavery to sin. Jesus says very clearly in John 8:34, "…everyone who commits sin is a slave to sin." Since everyone commits sin (Rom. 3:10-12), everyone is a slave to sin and a slave to the lies of the devil. Jesus said "You are of your father the devil, and your will is to do your father's desires" (John 8:44). We all are born, trapped to and bound by evil, sucked into the power of the evil one, and on our way to hell. We have rejected God's truth and embraced the lies of self-worship. We no longer live for the infinite God who made us but for the finite pleasure of self-seeking.

Though mankind is bound by the enemy's lies, praise God that there is hope of freedom and victory available. Jesus said in John 8:31-32, "If you abide in my word, you are truly my disciples, and you will know the truth, and the truth will set you free." Mankind is corrupt and continually captive to the lies of lust, pride, greed, and selfishness. In our daily self-seeking, we are deceived to believe the lie that true life and happiness are found in living for ourselves. Every day we feed on this lie and cannot escape its grasp on our lives. Yet here we see Jesus telling us that there is hope and freedom available from our bondage to self and the lie of self-seeking. If we abide in His Word, we will know the truth, and the truth will set us free. If we abide in Christ's words, we will know the truth, the truth that there is forgiveness for our sins, freedom from our bondage to self, victory over the evil one, and hope of eternal life found in Him. If we abide in God's Word, we will know the truth that Jesus is the Son of God who died, taking the punishment for our sins, and rose from the dead so that we may have true life.

It is this truth that will set us free, if we abide in it and truly believe it. Therefore, let go of the lies of the devil and believe in the truth of Christ revealed in God's Word. Nothing will fix your broken, empty, and corrupt life, except the truth of God's Word. This world offers many solutions to life's problems, but it is only God's divinely-inspired Word that will liberate you and take you into the reality of God's perfect everlasting love and grace. Without the truth of His Word, we remain forever bound and lost in the darkness of our sin.

Stopped Ears and Rebellious Hearts

As human beings, we often hear things that we do not want to hear or listen to. Someone may share with us a piece of honest criticism about a particular area of our life or challenge us to face some hard facts that we do not want to deal with. We can respond in several ways when this happens, often quite negatively. Many times children stop their ears with their fingers and start making loud humming noises so they cannot hear what one is saying. Adults generally will not do this but have other ways of responding to what has been said. They may ignore or pay little attention to what is being said or they may try to rationalize away the hard truths they have just encountered. The truth sometimes hurts and, because it hurts, people often respond negatively to it.

This is also the case when sinful man is faced with the truth of God revealed in Jesus Christ. Though God's truth brings life and freedom, sinful man does not listen to the truth but instead continues believing lies. In John 8, we see an example of this when Jesus confronts the Pharisees with the truth that He is the Messiah. In John 8:42-43, and 46-47 Jesus says, "If God were your Father, you would love me, for I came from God and I am here. I came not of my own accord, but he sent me. Why do you not understand what I say? It is because you cannot bear to hear my word. …If I tell the truth, why do you not believe me? Whoever is of God hears the words of God. The reason why you do not hear them is that you are not of God." In John 8, Jesus had been telling them the truth that He was the Messiah, the Savior, who had been sent by God the Father to this world to bring salvation. The Pharisees did not understand what Jesus was saying because they could not bear to hear the truth of His Word. They despised the truth of what He was saying to them, and so they stopped their ears and refused to listen.

A mark of those who do not know God is a failure to listen to the truth of Christ. Those who listen to and lovingly embrace the truth of Christ are the ones who truly know God. The problem with the Pharisees, religious as they were, is that they could not accept the truth that Jesus was the Messiah and Savior of the world. They could not face the fact that this lowly Jesus was the Son of God and Lord of the universe. They stopped their ears, shut up their hearts, and therefore kept themselves from truly knowing God.

Our postmodern pluralistic society is no different. The truth of Jesus being the only Savior and Lord has always been offensive to sinful man, but I believe this is especially the case in our pluralistic and relativistic culture. In a culture where all religions are equally valid and all roads lead in the same direction, the belief that there is only one truth and only one way to God is extremely offensive. The exclusivity of Christ goes against the stream of our Western culture, and there are few who dare follow it.

The heart of this rejection of the truth of Christ is sinful man's belief in the sovereignty of self. God is the sovereign all-powerful King and Ruler of all things, yet since the fall of man, all of mankind has a built-in desire and bent to rule and govern their own lives. God is the eternal, all-wise, all-knowing, all-powerful, always-present King, who rules with perfect love and justice, and yet sinful man rejects His good rule, spits in God's face, and says, "My way is better. I will run my life and determine what is good for me!" This is the heart of man's rejection of the truth of Christ.

Man in his sinful rebellion does not want to submit to God's truth but instead seeks to make his own truth. Sinful man says, "God is not the arbiter of truth; I am." Self is sovereign; God is not. That is why Paul, after urging Timothy to preach God's Word, warns him, saying, "For the time is coming when people will not endure sound teaching, but having itching ears they will accumulate for themselves teachers to suit their own passions, and will turn away from listening to the truth and wander off into myths" (2 Tim. 4:3-4). Paul warned Timothy that there was a time coming when people would turn away from God's truth and begin to make up their own "truth" based on their desires. Though this would have been a reality in Paul's time, it is especially a reality in our time.

We live in a society in which life is full of options. If you decide to go out to eat, you have a hundred different restaurants to select from. If you turn the TV on at home, you have a countless number of channels to preview. Whether in food, entertainment, fashion, technology, or education, our culture is full of options to choose from. We live in a consumerist culture, and this affects the way we approach religion and spirituality. People choose a religion that will best serve them and meet their desires. People mix and match different spiritualities and religious philosophies to satisfy their own passions and meet the standards they have in regards to what they think would be good for them. Man created in the image of God, is hungry for truth and meaning, but the distorted sovereign self that man has become has rejected God's truth and replaced it with a search to make his own truth and meaning. This is absurd and impossible!

The Coming Increase of Deception

As we have seen, mankind has been in bondage to sin and the lies of Satan ever since the fall of man in the Garden of Eden. Christ came to earth 2,000 years ago to defeat Satan, lift the curse of our condemnation, and free us from our bondage to the deceitfulness of sin. By faith in Him and what He did on the cross to save us, we are forgiven, declared right with God, and given the hope of eternal life with Him. Those who have put their trust in Jesus as their Savior and Lord are now children of God who have their eyes open to the beauty of God's truth revealed in His Word. Those who have not embraced Christ and His salvation are left in a state of bondage with the wrath of God upon them, waiting to be carried into eternal judgment when they die (John 3:36).

Through the death of Jesus on the cross, God judged the sins of His people and satisfied His just wrath towards their sin. Yet we await a future judgment day, when Christ will rid this earth of every evil residue and establish new heavens and a new earth where righteousness will dwell. At that time, He will throw every sinner who did not receive His mercy while alive into eternal punishment and will reward His people. God is just. There will be a final judgment where God's justice will have the last word. That day is coming soon.

The reason our world is so messed up is because it is still under the curse of sin. The Day of Judgment has not yet come. Lies still abound because that final day has not yet arrived. In fact, the Bible teaches that lies and deception will increase before the coming of Christ and the day of God's final judgment.

After being asked by His disciples what would be the sign of his coming and the close of the age, Jesus replies in Matt. 24:4-5: "See that no one leads you astray. For many will come in my name, saying, 'I am the Christ,' and they will lead many astray." As He continues to list the signs and events leading up to His coming He says again in v. 11, "And many false prophets will arise and lead many astray." Again in vs. 23-24 Jesus says, "Then if anyone says to you, 'Look, here is the Christ!' Or 'There he is!' do not believe it. For false christs and false prophets will arise and perform great signs and wonders, so as to lead astray, if possible, even the elect."

In Matthew 24:1-2, we see Jesus predict the destruction of the temple in Jerusalem which we know occurred in 70 A.D. So it seems that there was a partial fulfillment of the events described in Matthew 24 in the first century during the time of the destruction of the temple. But it seems that in this chapter as a whole, Jesus is describing signs and events that would immediately precede His Second Coming to the earth. This is the future fulfillment that we are still awaiting. This is consistent with what is called "the already but not yet" fulfillment of prophecy we see in the prophetic books of the Old Testament. In Scripture, we find that there are multiple fulfillments of prophecies. Concerning this latter fulfillment in Matt. 24, one of the pictures we see of the state of the world before His return is one of intense deception.

Jesus warns us three times in this chapter of the great deception that will infiltrate the human race in the last days. He says that many false christs and false prophets will arise and lead many astray. Many will claim to be the Christ, the Savior of the world. Many will claim to be the answer to the world's problems. They will even back up their claims with great signs and wonders. Their claims and miraculous signs will be so compelling and attractive that, if possible, it would lead the people of God astray. The lies will be so thick upon the earth that if it weren't for the sovereign grace of God, the people of God would themselves be deceived. That is why Jesus says in verse 22, "And if those days had not been cut short, no human being would be saved. But for the sake of the elect those days will be cut short."

These days of a great worldwide deception are coming. Ever since the fall of man, lies have covered the earth, but there is a time coming when the deception will increase to such a degree that it will almost lead the chosen people of God astray. That day is fast approaching. How will we as followers of Christ endure such great deception? The answer is that we must cling close to the truth of God's Word. We must love the truth with all of our heart. If we do not, we will fall and prove that we never truly knew Christ.

A Pre-tribulation Rapture? the Anti-Christ, and Discernment

At this point, many evangelical Christians would say, "I understand that we need to guard ourselves from false teaching, but we do not have to worry about this great time of deception that you speak of because the church will be secretly raptured (taken up with the Lord) before that time of great tribulation comes." This view is known as the pre-tribulation rapture. My response is that this view is completely unbiblical and finds no support in Scripture. To come to pre-tribulation conclusions, you have to read a meaning into the text that is simply not there. Nowhere does Scripture speak of a secret rapture before a tribulation period as though the Lord's coming were broken up into two parts. In Scripture you find the opposite picture. First Thessalonians 4:16-17 says, "For the Lord himself will descend from heaven with a cry of command, with the voice of an archangel, and with the sound of the trumpet of God. And the dead in Christ will rise first. Then we who are alive, who are left, will be caught up

together with them in the clouds to meet the Lord in the air…"
"Some hold that this will be secret, but Paul seems to be describing something open and public, with loud voices and a trumpet
blast."[8] Instead of a secret pre-tribulation rapture, this seems to
be an open and visible rapture which is connected to the literal
and physical appearing of the Lord Jesus descending from heaven
to earth. And Jesus only returns once, after the tribulation, not
twice (Matthew 24:29-31). Thus, believers are caught up to the
Lord after the tribulation when Jesus comes (v. 31). The reason
this needs to be stated so strongly is because many Christians will
not be ready for the great deception and suffering that will come
upon this earth if they are expecting a secret snatching up with
the Lord before the final tribulation begins.

One passage that will be helpful for us to look at is 2 Thessalonians 2:1-12. Here in this passage we see Paul instructing and
warning the Thessalonian Christians about what must take place
before Christ returns:

"Now concerning the coming of our Lord Jesus Christ and
our being gathered together to him, we ask you, brothers, not
to be quickly shaken in mind or alarmed, either by a spirit or a
spoken word, or a letter seeming to be from us, to the effect that
the day of the Lord has come. Let no one deceive you in any way.
For that day will not come, unless the rebellion comes first, and
the man of lawlessness is revealed, the son of destruction, who
opposes and exalts himself against every so-called god or object
of worship, so that he takes his seat in the temple of God, proclaiming himself to be God. Do you not remember that when I
was still with you I told you these things? And you know what is
restraining him now so that he may be revealed in his time. For
the mystery of lawlessness is already at work. Only he who now

---

8   Zondervan *NIV Study Bible* (Grand Rapids, MI: Zondervan, 2002), 1864.

restrains it will do so until he is out of the way. And then the lawless one will be revealed, whom the Lord Jesus will kill with the breath of his mouth and bring to nothing by the appearance of his coming. The coming of the lawless one is by the activity of Satan with all power and false signs and wonders, and with all wicked deception for those who are perishing, because they refused to love the truth and so be saved. Therefore God sends them a strong delusion, so that they may believe what is false, in order that all may be condemned who did not believe the truth but had pleasure in unrighteousness" (2 Thess. 2:1-12).

In refutation of the pre-tribulation view, John Piper commenting on this passage writes:

> "All pre-tribulationists believe that the man of lawlessness will be revealed after the rapture, during the great tribulation. In fact, they say that according to verses 6–7 the restrainer, which holds back the appearance of the man of lawlessness, is the Holy Spirit in the church, so that when the church is raptured out of the world, the man of lawlessness will be released. In other words, the church will not be here, they say, when the man of lawlessness is revealed. The Thessalonian Christians will not see the appearance of the man of lawlessness according to pre-tribulation teaching.
>
> "Why then would Paul try to convince them that the day of the Lord has not come by pointing out that a man of lawlessness has not been revealed whom they were never to see anyway? If Paul believed in a pre-tribulation rapture, all he had to say was: the day of the Lord can't have come yet because we are all still here. Instead what he does say is exactly what you would expect him to say

if he believed in a single post-tribulation coming of the Lord. He says that the day of the Lord can't be here yet because the apostasy and man of lawlessness who appears during the tribulation haven't appeared to us yet."[9]

I believe this careful observation by Piper is dead on and needs to be heeded. As long as we live in this present evil age, Christians will be called to patiently endure suffering in anticipation of the glorious appearing of Christ. We must realize this in order to truly persevere to the end.

That is why Jesus instructs us and warns us of the coming false prophets and false christs. That is why Paul instructs us and warns us of the coming of the Antichrist, the man of lawlessness. This world is full of deception; "the mystery of lawlessness is already at work" (2 Thess. 2:7). Yet there is a coming increase of deception that will arise upon this earth and shake up everything. It will be so intense that it would lead the elect astray if possible. How will we endure it if it comes in our lifetime? How can we be ready for this great deception and fight against it? We must love the truth.

In. 2 Thessalonians 2:9-10, we see that those who will be deceived by the Antichrist are those who refused to love the truth. Those who will be led astray by the mighty and spectacular miracles of the Antichrist will be those who refused to love the truth of God. Those who will not be able to see through the lies of his miracles will be those who don't cherish and cling to the Word of God with all of their hearts. Professing Christians will fall and be deceived if they do not delight in God's Word. You will be deceived, if you do not consider the Word of God precious treasure worth holding onto for dear life.

9 John Piper, "What Must Happen Before the Day of the Lord?" (Copyright August 30, 1987); available from www.desiringGod.org; accessed 17 December 2008. Used by permission.

An important realization is that there is a difference between merely believing the truth and loving the truth. You can believe with your head the facts of Scripture and have no genuine love for the truth you profess. Yet those who love the truth also love God and the Savior displayed in God's Word. Those who love the truth will not be deceived by the signs of the Antichrist because the signs of the Antichrist will not point people to Jesus. His signs will not point people to the glory of Christ and will not cultivate a deeper love for Christ. The Antichrist's signs will draw people away from Christ to worship him instead. True signs and wonders of God done by God's people will point people to the gospel of Jesus (Acts 14:3). Those who love the truth will recognize the difference.

In light of this great necessity to love the truth, I urge you to seek God in His Word and pray daily that He would grow your love for the truth. Begin cultivating the habit of sharing the truths of God's Word with those around you. Expose yourself to strong biblical teaching where God's Word is taught faithfully. Be committed to a local church that deeply values the truth of God's Word. This is important because though there will be a future increase of deception that will come before Christ's coming, we must also recognize the deception that is among us now.

False Teaching in the Church

Just because the Antichrist has not yet appeared and just because we have not yet entered into the great tribulation before Christ's return does not mean that we can loosen our grip on the truth and relax. We live in a continual and steady war where the truth is daily at stake. We encounter people on a daily basis who do not know God and who reject the truth of Christ. The truth is under constant attack from the outside world. Our culture is adamantly opposed to the idea of Christ being the only way to God. Our society is repulsed by the doctrine of hell and eternal judgment. Western man cringes at any moral stance concerning homosexuality and sex out of wedlock. The divine inspiration and authority of Scripture is considered a ridiculous idea to our postmodern world. The truth of Christ is under perpetual attack from the world in which we live.

This is a reality we must face in our daily battle for the truth, but there is an even more dangerous battle we must consider as we press forward in the Christian life. This battle is a battle we face on the inside. Lies and deception are not confined to the outside world but are constantly creeping into the church. And this reality of false teaching within the church is even more dangerous than the false teaching we encounter on the outside. John MacArthur writes: "Spiritual terrorists and saboteurs within the church pose a far more serious threat than manifestly hostile forces on the outside. From the very start of the church age, all the most spiritually deadly onslaughts against the gospel have come from people who pretended to be Christians—not from atheists and agnostics on the outside."[10]

Attacks against truth from outside the church often are like a man walking toward you with a large gun in his hand. You easily see it coming. Attacks against truth from inside the church often are like a deadly contagious virus that invisibly invades a body and slowly sucks the spiritual life out of its victims and those infected by them. It is more subtle.

Jude 4 explains this truth concerning false teaching: "For certain people have crept in unnoticed who long ago were designated for this condemnation, ungodly people, who pervert the grace of our God into sensuality and deny our only Master and Lord, Jesus Christ." Second Peter 2:1 is similar: "But false prophets also arose among the people, just as there will be false teachers among

---

10 John MacArthur, *The Truth War: Fighting for Certainty in an Age of Deception* (Nashville, TN: Nelson Books, 2007), 82.

you, who will *secretly* bring in destructive heresies." MacArthur points out the subtlety of false teachers by saying, "You can't necessarily tell a false teacher by the way he or she appears. Every false religious leader is, after all, 'religious' by definition. Looking saintly is practically part of the job description. Jesus referred to purveyors of false religion as wolves in sheep's clothing (Matthew 7:15), and 'whitewashed tombs…beautiful outwardly, but… full of dead men's bones and all uncleanness' (Matthew 23:27)."[11] MacArthur goes on to warn us that false teachers will have an appearance of spirituality and at times will sound very biblically based. Thus we must be alert to the great subtlety and danger of false teaching within the church.

The Emergent Church and the Repackaged Social Gospel of the Postmoderns

False teachings have come in various forms and ways throughout church history. I believe it is important to highlight here some of the false teachings we currently see in the Western church. One segment of false teaching that must be addressed is the teaching that is being spread within the emergent church. The emergent church is a movement within the church that has identified itself with postmodern culture and has taken on the postmodern mindset in order to reach out to today's prevailing culture. There are many good things emphasized within the emergent church. They talk much about community, social justice and following the ways of Jesus. But like most false teaching, they mix in truth with lies. Half-truths are indeed part of Satan's strategy in deceiving mankind (Gen. 3:5). Though there is some truth communicated by the emergent church, when it comes down to it, they have abandoned the foundational teachings of orthodox Christianity.

---

11 Ibid, 264.

There is much that could be pointed out as false in the emergent church, but the main flaw comes down to a distortion of two realities—truth and grace. Postmodernism is a worldview that rejects the belief in absolute truth and holds that the individual should seek to discover his or her own meaning in life. The emergent church and those of similar theology are taking this way of thinking and applying it to Christianity. Their attack on absolute truth and the *knowability* of truth can be seen in the following interview with Rob and Kristen Bell: "The Bells starting questioning their assumptions about the Bible itself—'discovering the Bible as a human product,' as Rob puts it, rather than the product of divine fiat. 'The Bible is still in the center for us,' Rob says, 'but it's a different kind of center. We want to embrace mystery, rather than conquer it.' 'I grew up thinking that we've figured out the Bible,' Kristen says, 'that we knew what it means. Now I have no idea what most of it means. And yet I feel like life is big again—like life used to be black and white, and now it's in color."[12]

Many in the emergent church deny that anyone can have certain knowledge about the truth, including what the Bible teaches. The conclusion that they draw is a denial of unchanging absolute truth. This is clearly expressed in the following words by Brian McLaren: "Our message and methodology have changed, do change, and must change if we are faithful to the ongoing and unchanging mission of Jesus Christ."[13] Here we see that for McLaren, the meaning of God's Word changes over time.

This denial of the existence of absolute unchanging truth and the *knowability* of that truth, has led the emergent church to distort the gospel of grace into a works-oriented salvation that fits more with postmodern culture (and ultimately with mankind in general). If the message of Scripture changes with the culture, then that

---

12 Andy Crouch, "The Emergent Mystique," *Christianity Today*, November 2004, 37-38.
13 Brian McLaren, *A Generous Orthodoxy* (Grand Rapids: Zondervan, 2004), 191.

means we need to reinterpret the Scriptures in a way that fits our culture. We are in a culture that sets a high value on open-mindedness and works of social justice but hates the concept of authority and divine judgment. Therefore, the emergent church pushes away the belief in the absolute unchanging authority of Scripture and the reality of eternal judgment and in exchange exalts the values of the culture, such as open mindedness and social justice. This leads to a distortion of the unchanging gospel of grace found in Christ alone. This is seen in the following quote by McLaren:

> "Although I don't hope all Buddhists will become (cultural) Christians, I do hope all who feel so called will become Buddhist followers of Jesus; I believe they should be given that opportunity and invitation. I don't hope all Jews or Hindus will become members of the Christian religion. But I do hope all who feel so called will become Jewish or Hindu followers of Jesus. Ultimately, I hope that Jesus will save Buddhism, Islam and every other religion, including the Christian religion, which often seems to need saving about as much as any other religion does. (In this context, I do wish all Christians would become followers of Jesus, but perhaps this is too much to ask. After all, I'm not doing such a hot job of it myself.)."[14]

For McLaren it does not matter what you believe about Jesus; it is only important that you live like Jesus. He believes you can be a good Hindu or Buddhist and be a follower of Jesus, by following the ways of Jesus.

MacArthur says of McLaren: "In the final analysis, he says, 'getting it right' is beside the point: the point is 'being and doing good'

---

14 Ibid, 264.

as followers of Jesus in our unique time and place, fitting in with the ongoing story of God's saving love for planet Earth."[15] For the emergent church, there is no clear teaching or emphasis on the gospel of God's saving grace found in Jesus Christ. The fact that man is born dead in sin, cut off from the Holy presence of God, and on the way to eternal hell has no part in the emergent church's theology. Man's desperate need of forgiveness and the hope of eternal life with God is not a clear focus for them. Jesus' penal, substitutionary death (Christ dying in our place and taking the penalty we deserved) is not in the forefront and is either denied totally or completely taken out of the picture. For the emergent church, "the cross is a moral example, 'showing God's loving heart, which wants forgiveness, not revenge, for everyone...The cross calls humanity to stop trying to make God's kingdom happen through coercion and force, which are always self-defeating in the end, and instead, to welcome it through self-sacrifice and vulnerability.'"[16]

The emergent church reduces the precious death of our Lord down to a mere moral example and blasphemously makes a mockery of what Christ accomplished and what it cost Him. The emergent church has distorted the gospel of God's rescuing grace given through the death and resurrection of Jesus by exchanging it for a social gospel that is out simply to promote peace, justice, and healing for the world. They have taken away the message of divine judgment and the heavy emphasis Scripture gives concerning the hope of eternal life which Christ died to accomplish. It is true that as Christians, we are called to seek peace and justice. These are good and biblical things. In fact, Jesus will one day restore the earth and establish perfect peace and justice. But the huge flaw of the emergent church is that they have placed social justice as the

---

15 MacArthur, *Truth War*, 36.
16 Kevin DeYoung and Ted Kluck, *Why We're Not Emergent (By Two Guys Who Should Be)*, (Chicago, IL: Moody Publishers, 2008), 193.

ultimate good news and completely pushed away the central message of the atonement along with the eternal perspective given throughout all of Scripture. The problem is, "Emergent leaders are hoping for heaven on earth before Jesus returns to earth to bring the new heaven and new earth. Emergent leaders dare us to imagine a world without poverty and war and injustice. That's good. We need to be stirred to have faith in the God of the impossible. But we should not expect something God has not promised, especially when He has promised the opposite. Jesus said the poor would always be with us (John 12:8) and wars and rumors of war would continue to the very end (Matt. 24:6)."[17]

God calls and uses us as Christians to bring change to the world, but we will not be the ones who ultimately fix our broken lives and this broken world by our good works. Our world is cursed, we are sinners, and Jesus alone is the mighty and gracious Savior who died, rose again, and is coming back to judge the wicked, restore the earth, and lavish His love upon His Bride, the church, forever.

This is a warning to all those who are being led astray by the teachings of the emergent church. It is a serious matter because these teachings are not just confined within the emergent church. This repackaged social gospel of the postmoderns is being pushed in many evangelical circles within the Western church. Be discerning and watchful. It smells like trouble anytime social justice is the central focus of a church, organization, or movement. Do not get me wrong, as Christians we must pursue social justice. A large amount of Scripture is given that strictly obligates us to take care of the poor and oppressed. But the central message of Scripture is God's saving grace given through the Person and redeeming work of Jesus Christ. If you put social justice before the mes-

17 Ibid, 187.

sage of grace, you are headed in the wrong direction. This is not an either/or between social justice and grace. But the simple fact is that the gospel of grace found in Christ must be front and center. The centrality of grace leads us to do works of social justice, but the centrality of social justice never leads us to cling closer to God's grace. Instead, it puts us in danger of moving further away from it, into the deadly trap of self-righteousness. Reconciliation between God and sinful man must come before reconciliation between sinful man and sinful man. This is the divine order that all of Scripture gives us (Mark 12:28-31).

The Prosperity Gospel and Other Distortions

I grew up living on the Gulf Coast of Mississippi. The coast is known for various things, but one aspect of coastal life that is well known is the casino industry. There are several casinos lined up across the waterways of southern Mississippi. When people go to the casinos they bring money, hoping to come away with more money. They put their quarters into the slot machines hoping that hundreds or thousands will come out. There is a type of teaching infiltrating the Western church that treats God like a divine slot-machine who always brings a return. This teaching says that, if you follow Jesus, obey God and pay your tithe to the church, God is going to bless you with health, wealth and prosperity. This teaching has been referred to as "the prosperity gospel."

First, we must acknowledge that Scripture does teach that God will provide for his people. Yet it is clear that God's provision does not equal being made rich. In Matthew 6, after Jesus tells us not to worry about our basic needs, such as food, drink, and clothing, He goes on in verse 33 to say, "Seek first the kingdom of God and his righteousness, and all these things will be added to you." He does not say, "seek first the kingdom of God, and you will be rich." He says that if we seek first God's kingdom, God will add all these things (food, drink, and clothing) to us. He will provide for our basic needs.

Those who teach following God automatically equals becoming healthy, wealthy, prosperous and free from suffering are going directly against clear biblical teaching. God can and does bless Christians with great financial resources but primarily for the purpose of enabling them to be a blessing to others and help spread the message of the gospel. The overwhelming perspective we get from the Bible, especially the New Testament, is that God's people will not escape the troubles of this world but will be called to suffer. Acts 14:22 says that "through many tribulations we must enter the kingdom of God." Jesus Himself was poor and suffered much, even to the point of the excruciating death on the cross. His disciples would follow in His footsteps (Matt. 10:17-18, 24-25; Matt. 16:24-26; Luke 12:33; John. 16:33). First Peter says a lot about suffering, and (in 4:19) it is clear that suffering is a part of God's will for His people.

The problem with the prosperity gospel is that it teaches people to *use* God in order that they might get what their selfish, greedy hearts want. Instead of wanting and desiring God for who He is, they want God for what He can give them. They step on the giver in order to get the gift. They do not love God, but they use God to get to the god they truly love: money. Paul himself in 1 Timothy 6 warns those who use the Christian life as a means to financial gain. He speaks of these people as ones who believe "that godliness is a means of gain" (v. 5). In 6:6-10 he states, "Now there is great gain in godliness with contentment, for we brought nothing into the world, and we cannot take anything out of the world. But if we have food and clothing, with these we will be content. But those who desire to be rich fall into temptation, into a snare, into many senseless and harmful desires that plunge people into ruin and destruction. For the love of money is a root of all kinds of evils. It is through this craving that some have wandered away from the faith and pierced themselves with many pangs."

From this passage, we see that as Christians we are to be content with our basic needs of food and clothing. Paul warns us that the mere desire to be rich leads to ruin and destruction. Desiring prosperity and using the Christian life as a means to getting it leads to nothing but danger. Through this craving, many wander away from the truth of the gospel. Christ died to save us and free us from the idolatry of wealth so that we may love and serve Him. Jesus reminds us, "No one can serve two masters, for either he will hate the one and love the other, or he will be devoted to the one and despise the other. You cannot serve God and money" (Matt. 6:24). If we try to use Him as a means of getting money, we are expressing hatred for Him and wandering from the truth.

Other distortions that are sometimes connected to prosperity teaching would be those within the charismatic movement (that emphasize and pursue the supernatural gifts of the Holy Spirit such as prophecy, tongues, and healing). Let me say that I believe there are some charismatic churches that are more biblical than others. By no means am I against the biblical teaching of the supernatural gifts of the Holy Spirit. But in a good number of charismatic churches, there is much imbalanced teaching that strays away from the truth of God's Word. I am not pointing out flaws in the charismatic movement just to criticize but out of a desire to see its renewal.

The first significant observation I see within a large part of the charismatic church is an unbiblical Holy Spirit centeredness rather than a more biblical Christ-centeredness. Scripture teaches that there is one God who exists in three persons, Father, Son, and Holy Spirit. All persons of the Trinity are equal in essence, that is, they are equal in power and glory. Scripture also teaches that each member of the Trinity relates differently to one another. Though equal in essence, the Father has authority over the Son and Holy Spirit (Jn. 3:16, 5:19, 14:26). The Son submits to the will of the Father (Jn. 5:30) and the Holy Spirit proceeds from the Father and Son (Jn. 15:26, 16:7). The Son was sent to the earth to glorify the Father and in turn the Father glorified His Son (John 17:1-5).

We also see that the Holy Spirit was sent to glorify Jesus. Speaking of the Holy Spirit in John 16:14 Jesus said, "He will glorify me." Again in John 15:26 Jesus speaking of the Holy Spirit said, "…he will bear witness about me." The role of the Holy Spirit is to point people to Jesus and to magnify Jesus. The Spirit brings glory to Jesus by pointing people to Him, His gospel, and the effects of His gospel.

The problem with much (not all) of the charismatic movement is that its churches are more centered on the Holy Spirit than on Jesus. As Christians, we are by no means to neglect or deemphasize the Holy Spirit (much of the church needs to be cautious of this). Yet we must recognize that the Holy Spirit's role is to point people to Jesus, not to Himself. If there is much talk about the Holy Spirit and many wonders are supposedly done in the power of the Spirit and yet no attention is given to Jesus, it is not a move of God. The Holy Spirit always points people to Jesus and His redemptive work. Jesus speaking about the Holy Spirit says in John 16:8-11, "…he will convict the world concerning sin and righteousness and judgment: concerning sin, because they do not believe in me; concerning righteousness, because I go to the Father, and you will see me no longer; concerning judgment, because the ruler of this world is judged." The Holy Spirit's convicting work is directly related to pointing out unbelief and illuminating minds to the saving righteousness and victory given through Christ's death and resurrection.

The outpouring of the Holy Spirit at Pentecost in Acts 2, which resulted in the supernatural ability to speak in other languages, was a miraculous sign that testified to the power and validity of the gospel of Jesus preached by Peter that led thousands to faith in Christ. The signs and wonders done by the apostles through the power of the Holy Spirit bore witness to the truth of God's grace found in Jesus (Acts. 14:3). The work of the Spirit is to draw attention to Christ and His great work of salvation, thus bringing Christ glory. Charismatic churches need to test and see where they stand with this reality.

Another problem in many charismatic churches is an emphasis on the miraculous work of the Spirit (tongues, healing, prophecy, etc.) over and above the sanctifying work of the Spirit. Paul says in 1 Cor. 13:1-3, "If I speak in the tongues of men and of angels, but have not love, I am a noisy gong or a clanging cymbal. And if I have prophetic powers, and understand all mysteries and all knowledge, and if I have all faith, so as to remove mountains, but have not love, I am nothing." The miraculous gifts are pointless if there is no love coming from that person. Love is primary; miraculous gifts are secondary.

The miraculous gifts of the Spirit are not an end in themselves. True Christ-honoring miracles are meant to point people to greater growth in holiness. Miraculous gifts are not meant to excite people and to be exercised as some kind of show. They are for the edification of the church. "...The one who prophesies speaks to people for their upbuilding and encouragement and consolation" (1 Cor. 14:3). Godliness and love for God come before and are more important than miraculous gifts of the Spirit. Christ-likeness is the goal and should be the main focus. The miraculous gifts are the servant of this goal.

Though there are other concerns, the last problem that I believe needs to be addressed concerning the charismatic movement is their failure to bring together the Word and Spirit. Though most in the charismatic movement believe in the divine inspiration and authority of Scripture, many act as though they are more guided and reliant upon their emotions, experiences, and supernatural encounters, than God's Word. This should not be the case.

Second Timothy 3:16-17 states, "All Scripture is breathed out by God and profitable for teaching, for reproof, for correction, and for training in righteousness, that the man of God may be competent, equipped for every good work." Paul also commands ministers: "preach the word; be ready in season and out of season; reprove, rebuke, and exhort, with complete patience and teaching" (2 Tim. 4:2). The Bible is the divinely inspired Word of God that we must have if we are going to be equipped for every good work. God's Word and the preaching of God's Word must be central in the life of every individual Christian and church. Supernatural experiences and the miraculous work of the Spirit emphasized above the Word of God will leave people vulnerable to much error because they are not guarded by the unchanging truth. The Holy Spirit is called the Spirit of truth and is the One who leads us to a growing understanding of and obedience to God's Word. The Spirit and the Word are meant to work together, not separately. This is an area of much-needed renewal in the charismatic movement.

The Minimization of Truth

False teaching and distortions of the truth are not the only danger the church faces. A potentially more predominant reality for the Western church is a growing minimization of truth. Instead of corrupting the truth, many evangelical churches are simply putting truth on the back burner. Their doctrinal statement may be in line with orthodox evangelical Christianity, but in practice they show themselves to deny the doctrines they profess. In trying to reach the culture and be relevant, many evangelical churches have watered down the truth of God's Word. Instead of changing the truth entirely to fit the culture like the emergents, they have merely diluted and deemphasized certain aspects of it.

At first glance, it is not their message that has changed but only their methodology or the way they communicate that message. It is definitely true that we as Christians will be called to communicate in ways that will be understandable to the culture we are trying to reach. All missionaries know that believers must be able to speak the unchanging truth of the gospel in a contextually understandable way to the culture they are engaging. But this must not come at the cost of watering down the message in any way. If the message is watered down, then the methodology you are using is flawed.

Though we need to communicate the truth in a culturally understandable way, there will be times when we need to confront the flaws of the culture. Currently, we live in an entertainment and image-based ADD culture. David Wells elaborates by saying, "This is a video-crazed, image-driven, picture-conscious culture, not a literate one. Our minds are entirely inert, lifeless, and useless until prodded into action by the sight of something eye-popping. Images are the fuel that, when injected into the motor, kick it all into life. Without them our minds are as limp as deflated balloons."[18]

Images and pictures are not inherently bad, and there will be times when we can use these culturally relevant ways of communication to reach out with the truth. But if this culture is driven by images to the point that it is no longer able to rigorously engage the mind with the reading, studying and hearing of God's Word, then we need to confront and challenge the culture.

The problem with many evangelical churches is that they have observed the entertainment drive of our culture and, in an effort

---

18 David Wells, *Courage to Be Protestant*, 24.

to reach out to people, have adapted their churches and ministries to be entertainment-based. In the process of doing this they have minimized and watered down the hard truths of Scripture. They have fed the superficial and consumerist heart of Western people, leaving them no different, instead of challenging and exhorting them with what they really need in order to change—the hard unchanging truths of God's Word. When our minds and churches no longer have an appetite for deep truth, that is when we must break from the ways of our culture and seek desperately for a renewal of love for the truth of God's Word. The truth is what our world really needs. May God grace the evangelical church to take people of our entertainment culture beyond the surface into the deep, endless, life-changing waters of God's truth.

The Cure against Lies and False Teaching: Stay Close to the Gospel

In the medical world, harmful and deadly diseases are encountered everyday. For doctors to successfully fight these diseases in their patients, they must have some sort of cure or be able to perform a medical procedure that has been known to work. When encountering the lies of this world and the false teachings within the church, we also must be equipped with the cure that will guard us from harm and danger. Seeking and having an understanding of the whole counsel of God's Word is of upmost importance in guarding us from deception. Of particular significance in our battle for the truth is the importance of staying close to the gospel of Jesus Christ. The gospel and its centrality is the cure against false teaching. Keeping central in our hearts and lives what the Scriptures keep central, namely the person and saving work of Jesus Christ, will keep us from great error. If we keep the main thing the main thing, we will guard ourselves from the danger of wandering from the faith.

Paul tells us what it is that should be central in our lives as Christians: "I would remind you, brothers, of the gospel I preached to you…For I delivered to you as of first importance what I also received: that Christ died for our sins in accordance with the Scriptures, that he was buried, that he was raised on the third day in accordance with the Scriptures," (1 Cor. 15:1, 3-4). The saving work of Jesus Christ is of first importance and must be kept central in our lives. The gospel of God's saving grace given to sinners through the death and resurrection of Jesus must be the prevailing focus of our hearts and minds throughout our whole lives. This was the driving force of Paul's life and ministry. In 1 Cor. 2:2 he states, "For I decided to know nothing among you except Jesus Christ and him crucified."

This matter is so serious that turning from or distorting the gospel results in eternal condemnation. Paul says in Gal. 1:8-9, "But even if we or an angel from heaven should preach to you a gospel contrary to the one we preached to you, let him be accursed. As we have said before, so now I say again: If anyone is preaching to you a gospel contrary to the one you received, let him be accursed." The gospel Paul preached communicated that "For our sake he (God the Father) made him (Jesus, God's Son) to be sin (take on our sin and be punished for it) who knew no sin, so that in him we might become the righteousness of God." (2 Cor. 5:21) This gospel is again communicated in Rom. 3:23-26, "…for all have sinned and fall short of the glory of God, and are justified by his grace as a gift, through the redemption that is in Christ Jesus, whom God put forward as a propitiation (wrath removing sacrifice) by his blood, to be received by faith. This was to show God's righteousness, because in his divine forbearance he had passed over former sins. It was to show his righteousness at the present time, so that he might be just and the justifier of the one who has faith in Jesus."

This same gospel is communicated in 1 Peter 3:18 which states: "For Christ also suffered once for sins, the righteous for the unrighteous, that he might bring us to God." We are sinners separated and condemned before a Holy God. He sent His divine Son Jesus to this earth to be born a man, to live the perfect life we could not, to die the death we deserved and to rise again, so that by faith in Him we may be right with God and restored to eternal fellowship with Him. To preach a gospel contrary to this results in eternal judgment. To guard ourselves and those around us from lies and false teaching, we must cling to the true gospel of Jesus Christ. Not doing so will lead to greater vulnerability and susceptibility in being deceived. Clinging closely to the gospel is the cure and will be the cure as the deception increases upon this earth in the coming days.

A Word to Dead Orthodoxy

In this chapter, we have focused on the importance of loving the truth, especially as the deception increases upon the earth leading up to the return of Christ. As false teaching and lies prevail outside and within the church, we must learn to cling closely to God's Word and the gospel of Jesus that it declares. But also of importance is that mere knowledge of the facts of Scripture and the gospel do not equate with a love for the truth. James 2:19 says, "Even the demons believe—and shudder!" The demons believe and probably have more knowledge than most Christians, but this does not mean that they love God. They hate the truth and they hate the God of truth. Many professing Christians may be very orthodox in their theology and even love to study the Bible and yet have a dead and cold heart that feels no true love for God.

God's Word is not an end in itself; it points us to life found in a person and that person is Jesus Christ. In John 5:39-40 Jesus speaking to those who were religious says, "You search the Scriptures because you think that in them you have eternal life; and it is they that bear witness about me, yet you refuse to come to me that you may have life." Jesus tells religious people that if you look to the Bible as an end in itself to give life, you are on the wrong track. The Scriptures are words of life but only because they point us to the glorious Son of God, Jesus Christ, who gives us true and eternal life with God. We come to the Bible so that ultimately we may come to Christ, who gives us life. True Christianity is about an intimate love relationship with the triune God, who is Father, Son, and Holy Spirit. You might know the Bible like the back of your hand, but if you are not growing in deep affection and desire for God, then your Christianity is in danger of freezing to death. It is dangerous to have a warm head and a cold heart. People who truly love the truth are those who seek God's Word so that they may grow in joyous worship and loving obedience to their great God and Savior. Examine yourself and test whether you actually love the truth. Pray that God may revive your heart.

Expressing Love for the Truth

Just as there are many ways to express your love for someone, there are many ways to express your love for the truth, which ultimately is an expression of love for the God of truth. One way to express (and to grow in) love for the truth is to spend much time reading, studying, and hearing the truth of God's Word. We tend to spend the most amount of time doing the things we love. Spending time reading and studying the Bible daily is one way of expressing love for the truth. The psalmist expressed his love for God's Word by spending much time in it. As Psalm 119:97 states, "Oh how I love your law! It is my meditation all the day." Attentively and desirously sitting under and listening to the faithful preaching of God's Word is also a great indicator and expression of a growing love for the truth.

Another way to express love for the truth is to boldly proclaim the truth. Paul gives us an example of this boldness in his statement in Romans 1:16 by saying, "I am not ashamed of the gospel, for it is the power of God for salvation to everyone who believes...." Paul was not ashamed of the gospel and the truth of God's Word. He endured much persecution and gave his whole life to proclaiming it no matter the cost. The book of Acts is full of countless examples of people in the early church who boldly proclaimed the truth even when it was not well received.

Yet another expression of love for the truth is found in Paul's statement to the Ephesian elders in Acts 20:27: "I did not shrink from declaring to you the whole counsel of God." A mark of someone who loves the truth of God's Word is one who will not pick and choose only the parts of Scripture that they like but will proclaim all that it teaches, even the hard parts. Pastors who love the Word of God will proclaim the whole counsel of God's Word and will not hold back the difficult teachings of Scripture. Those who genuinely love the truth will believe all that Scripture teaches and will submit in belief even to the aspects that confront their differing preconceived ideas.

A difficult and yet essential expression of love for the truth is the confronting of false teaching. True love is expressed by protecting that which you love. If a husband truly loves his wife, he will seek to ward off any intruders into the home that would try to bring harm. Loving the truth of God's Word results in seeking to protect that truth. We protect the truth of God's Word by exposing and refuting false teaching. God's Word commands us to do this. We are called "to contend for the faith" (Jude 3). Most of the New Testament epistles in some form deal directly with confronting specific false teachings encountered within the church. In Jeremiah 28 and 29:24–32, we see two specific examples of

Jeremiah confronting false prophecy given to God's people. We show honor and love for the God we serve by protecting the truth of His Word given to us.

A Word to Leaders in the Church

In light of the serious reality concerning false teaching and the minimization of truth that plagues the church, leaders within the church will be called to a greater degree of accountability. James 3:1 says, "Not many of you should become teachers, my brothers, for you know that we who teach will be judged with greater strictness." Luke 12:48 also says, "Everyone to whom much was given, of him much will be required." Leaders and teachers within the church have been given great gifts and responsibilities by God, which are not to be taken lightly. Leaders have the serious task of watching over souls; they will be accountable to God concerning how well they took care of them (Heb. 13:17). Leaders have the great responsibility of faithfully preaching the gospel (Acts 20:21, 24), declaring the whole counsel of God's Word (Acts 20:27), guarding and protecting God's people from false teaching (Acts 20:28-31), equipping believers for ministry (Eph. 4:11-12) and bringing the body of Christ to fullness of maturity in Christ (Eph. 4:11-14). Pastors and leaders in the church will have to stand before God, look Him in the eye, and give an account for the way they cared for the church. This is a daunting and sobering reality. May God bring a renewal of truth-loving leaders within the church who faithfully lead God's people into a deeper love for the truth, resulting in greater love for the God who *is* truth.

Godliness is the Greatest Expression and Indicator of those who Love the Truth

In reality, a person could study the Bible daily, boldly proclaim the truth, and confront false teaching and yet not truly love the God of truth. We see this in Revelation 2:2, 4 in Jesus' confrontation with the church in Ephesus. He says, "I know your works, your toil and your patient endurance, and how you cannot bear with those who are evil, but have tested those who call themselves apostles and are not, and found them to be false.... But I have this against you, that you have abandoned the love you had at first." This church confronted false teaching and stood up for the truth of God's Word and yet had abandoned their love for God and one another. Jesus called them—and calls us—to repent of this disconnect.

True love for God's truth is expressed in walking in love for God and our neighbor. Those who truly love the truth of God's Word love, worship, and obey the God who has brought them into the truth of His love and grace. Godly living is the greatest expression and indicator of love for God's truth. Titus 1:1 tells us that "knowledge of the truth...accords with godliness." True knowledge of and love for God's Word must always lead to godly living.

A Call to Love the Truth in the Midst of Increasing Deception

In this chapter we have talked about what is of upmost importance for all Christians in order to have a growing love for the truth of God's word. This is especially important the closer we get to the return of our Lord Jesus. The more lies that abound, the closer we will have to cling to the truth. Our world is full of lies and deception of all sorts, but there is a day coming when the deception will increase and become so strong that almost the entire world will be led astray. God's people themselves would be led astray if possible. Only by God's sovereign grace will His people be able to endure such great evil. This is a call to cling tightly to the Word of God. This is a call to grow in your love for the truth. This is a call to prepare for what is to come.

CHAPTER 3

Be Holy

It is not enough simply to have a love for ideas, conceptions, and doctrine if those ideas, conceptions, and doctrines do not truly take root in the conviction of the heart, resulting in the sprouting of a changed life. Developing a true love for the truth means that the seed of God's Word is sinking deeper and deeper into the fertile soil of one's heart and bringing forth more and more fruit of a changed life. True love for the truth encompasses the mind and the heart and results in the inward and outward transformation of the person. This is wrought in believers by the supernatural work of the Holy Spirit as they pursue and seek God through His Word with much diligence and prayer.

As we prepare for our Lord's coming, we must love and seek the truth in such a way that we are continually increasing and growing in godly living before the Lord. God calls every Christian to this way of life, and as the days grow darker this will be an even greater challenge. Along with the coming increase of deception before the return of Jesus will come an increase in ungodliness. The more gasoline you spread across a fire, the greater the flames will rise. The more lies spread throughout the earth, the greater the flames of ungodliness will arise.

The Coming Increase of Lawlessness

In reference to the end times Jesus says in Matthew 24:12, "And because lawlessness will be increased, the love of many will grow cold." Verse 11 speaks of the increase of deception upon the earth, and from that increase of deception the increase in lawlessness comes. Before the return of Jesus, there will be an increase in ungodliness across the earth. Mankind will walk in a heightened disobedience and rebellion to God's law. In our sinful nature, we are capable of much more evil than what we currently demonstrate. The only reason the world is not expressing more evil than it currently does is because God is restraining it from the fullness of its potential. In the coming days, God's restraining leash upon the world will be let loose and the sexual immorality, greed, pride, and violence of man will run rampant like never before in this world's history. The love of many will grow cold. Man's hearts will be frozen in hatred and immorality (Matt. 24:10, 12) and their words and actions will be packed with greater bitterness and perversion.

Second Timothy 3:1-5 gives us the same picture of the end times: "But understand this, that in the last days there will come times of difficulty. For people will be lovers of self, lovers of money, proud, arrogant, abusive, disobedient to their parents, ungrateful, unholy, heartless, unappeasable, slanderous, without self-control, brutal, not loving good, treacherous, reckless, swollen with conceit, lovers of pleasure rather than lovers of God, having the appearance of godliness, but denying its power." These characteristics of man can be found throughout the course of history. But there will be a greater intensification of these sins in the time before Christ's return. People will have an obsessive and uncontrollable love for self, money, and pleasure. They will have no love for God or for what is good. They will love evil and be addicted to everything that is wicked. Their lives will be dominated by idolatry, and their hearts will be full of pride, hatred, and deception, resulting in an overflow of all sorts of rebellion. In the midst of such wickedness, they will try to put on a disguise of religiosity and morality, thus demonstrating their ridiculous hypocrisy. Such will be the case before Christ returns.

The Holy Nature of God

Though mankind is sinful and in the coming days that sinfulness will increase, we know that this is not the case with God. God is Holy. He is completely unstained, separate from sin, and exalted above this ungodly world. This is what is meant when it is said that God is holy. Jerry Bridges describes God's holiness this way: "Holiness describes both the majesty of God and the purity and moral perfection of His nature."[19]

In Scripture, God is seen as the majestic King that is exalted above all. We see this in Isaiah 6:1-3 as Isaiah the prophet writes: "In the year King Uzziah died I saw the Lord sitting upon a throne, high and lifted up; and the train of his robe filled the temple. Above him stood the seraphim. Each had six wings: with two he covered his face, and with two he covered his feet, and with two he flew. And one called to another and said: 'Holy, holy, holy is the Lord of hosts; the whole earth is full of his glory!'"

In Isaiah's vision of the Lord, he sees God high and lifted up as the majestic King over all. Even these glorious heavenly beings are humbled by His greatness as they cover their faces and feet. Stunned, they cry out 'Holy, holy, holy is the Lord of hosts; the whole earth is full of his glory!' Their cries ascribing the Lord as thrice holy convey the incomparable majesty and perfection of His being. This same truth is exemplified in Exodus 15:11 when Moses says "Who is like you, O Lord, among the gods? Who is like you, majestic in holiness...?"

The fact that God is exalted in majesty over all also means that He is completely separate from sin. First John 1:5 says, "God is light, and in him is no darkness at all." Habakkuk 1:13 says that

---

19 Jerry Bridges, *The Pursuit of Holiness* (Colorado Springs, CO: NavPress, 1978), 22.

God is "of purer eyes than to see evil and cannot look at wrong."
He is described in Isaiah 5:16 as "the Holy God" who "shows
himself holy in righteousness." God is the exalted and majestic
King who is completely separate from all that is evil and impure.
He shows Himself holy in righteousness. His holiness means that
He always does what is right and is completely pure and morally
excellent in every possible way.

God Created Man in His Likeness

Genesis 1:27 tells us that "God created man in his own image,
in the image of God he created him; male and female he created
them." Much could be said in regard to what this means exactly,
but one aspect of what it means to be created in the image of
God is that we were created as moral creatures. In Genesis 2:16-
17 we see God giving man a command: "You may surely eat of
every tree of the garden, but of the tree of the knowledge of good
and evil you shall not eat, for in the day that you eat of it you
shall surely die." Man was created in the image of God as a moral
creature. Man was created to love God, obey God, and be holy,
as God is holy. Ephesians 4:24 describes what it means to have
the image of God restored in us as fallen creatures as we come to
know Jesus:"put on the new self, created after the likeness of God
in true righteousness and holiness."To be created in the image of
God and to be restored to the image of God through faith in Jesus
means to walk in holiness.

As human beings it is evident that we bear the resemblance of
our parents in various ways. Stubbornness seems to be a typical
Wilburn family trait which appears to have been passed on from
my dad to me. Just as we bear the likeness of our earthly fathers,
we too were created to bear the likeness of our Heavenly Father,
which means that we are to be holy as He is holy.

The Substance of Holiness

As we looked at what it means that God is holy and recognized that we were created to be holy as He is holy, it is important now that we dig in more deeply to see what the nature and substance of personal holiness is. In light of our call as Christians to walk in holiness as we prepare for the Lord's coming, we need to understand more of what that means. J. C. Ryle defines personal holiness this way: "Holiness is the habit of being of one mind with God, according as we find His mind described in Scripture. It is the habit of agreeing in God's judgment, hating what He hates, loving what He loves, and measuring everything in this world by the standard of His Word. He who most entirely agrees with God, he is the most holy man. A holy man will endeavor to shun every known sin and to keep every known commandment. He will have a decided bent of mind towards God, a hearty desire to do His will, a greater fear of displeasing Him than of displeasing the world, and a love to all His ways..."[20]

In essence, walking in holiness means "hating what He hates" and "loving what He loves." To be holy as God is holy, is to hate what God hates and love what God loves. In Leviticus 19:2 God says very clearly, "Be holy because I, the Lord your God, am holy." In context to this command, God gives many different laws for the nation of Israel to follow. So to be holy means to conform to the character of God by following the laws of God. Jesus comes along many years later and sums up all the laws of the Old Testament in two commands: "'You shall love the Lord your God with all your heart and with all your soul and with all your mind and with all your strength.'... 'You shall love your neighbor as yourself'" (Mk. 12:30-31).

Thus we see that the essence of holiness is love. To be holy is to love God with your whole being and to love your neighbor as

---

20 J.C. Ryle, *Holiness: Its Nature, Hindrances, Difficulties, and Roots* (Peabody, MA: Hendrickson Publications, 2007), 44.

yourself. To be holy is to love what God loves. God loves and up-holds His glory. Romans 11:36 says, "For from him and through him and to him are all things. To him be glory forever. Amen." As Christians, we are to share in this love and passion for the glory of God. To walk in holiness means that our whole life is wrapped up in a single relentless pursuit of bringing praise, worship, and honor to the one who created us and saved us. We bring glory to Him by loving Him with all our heart, soul, mind, and strength and loving our neighbor as ourselves.

We bring glory to God when we love Him with all our desires, thoughts, and actions. To love God is to have deep desire, longing, and affection for God, overflowing with joy in God. To love God is to meditate continually on His greatness, thinking right thoughts of Him and His Word. To love God is to do every action according to His Word and unto His honor. Love for God ultimately is expressed when our lives revolve more and more around our glorious Savior, Jesus, and everything we do is done to exalt Him.

Love for God is expressed when we love people because we know that God loves people. If we do not love people, it proves we do not love God. First John 4:20 states, "If anyone says, 'I love God,' and hates his brother, he is a liar; for he who does not love his brother whom he has seen cannot love God whom he has not seen." God calls us to walk with kindness, gentleness, and patience toward our neighbor. He calls us to help those who are poor and in need and to be humble servants of those all around us. We must love people as an expression of our love for God because God loves people. Thus, to be holy means to love what God loves.

To be holy not only means to love what God loves but also to hate what God hates. Like a young boy who roots for the sports team his father likes and cheers against the sports teams his father dislikes, we too as God's children are to be for what He is for and to be against what He is against. True love for God equals a hatred for the things that are contrary to God. Proverbs 8:13 states, "The fear of the Lord is hatred of evil." To truly fear, to truly reverence and adore God, automatically means you will hate and turn from all that is opposed to the pure and holy God who is love. Since God is pure, holy, just and loving, we as His followers must be against all that is impure, unholy, unjust, and unloving. Since God is against pride, greed, lust, lies, idolatry, and evil in its every form, we too as His people must be against pride, greed, lust, lies, idolatry, and evil in its every form. Every prideful thought is to be repulsed. Every selfish desire is to taste bitter to the soul. Every impure word is to be treated with disgust. Every unloving action is to make the heart cringe. Every ounce of evil is to be despised and forsaken.

Psalm 97:10 says, "O you who love the Lord, hate evil!" Romans 12:9 says "Abhor what is evil; hold fast to what is good." To deeply and passionately love God means to deeply and passionately hate all that is not found in the heart of God. Just as a bear robbed of her cub is filled with vehement rage and fierce anger, we too should be filled with the same intense rage and striking anger toward anything (not anyone) that would rob God of the honor He deserves.

Scripture teaches that it is impossible to love God if instead of hating the things God hates we love those very things He hates. First John 2:15-17 states, "Do not love the world or the things in the world. If anyone loves the world, the love of the Father is not in him. For all that is in the world—the desires of the flesh and the desires of the eyes and the pride in possessions—is not from the Father but is from the world. And the world is passing away along with its desires, but whoever does the will of God abides forever." If you love the things of this world, if you love the lust and pride of this world, you will not be able to love God. Thomas Watson writes, "Christ is never loved till sin be loathed. Heaven is never longed for till sin be loathed."[21] Sin must be hated and forsaken if we are to grow in love for Christ and longing for Heaven.

Thus, to be holy is to love what God loves and to hate what God hates. To be holy is to love and cherish the glory and honor of God and to spit upon, turn from, and despise all that devalues and dishonors God (meaning all that is sinful, not the sinner). This is the substance of personal holiness.

Our Failure and God's Restoring Work

Though God is holy and man was created to be holy, since the fall of man all of humanity has become unholy. All of us have failed to love God and our neighbor as we should. We have rebelled against the holy God and rejected His holy ways. The image of God within each one of us has become corrupt and defiled, thus leaving us cut off from His holy presence. The beautiful innocence, purity and love that was once ours as we dwelt in perfect intimacy with God in the garden has been shattered. This is a great tragedy.

The good news is that God had a plan from the beginning, even from eternity, to restore rebellious man to true holiness. Ephesians 1:3-4 states, "Blessed be the God and Father of our Lord Jesus Christ, who has blessed us in Christ with every spiritual blessing in the heavenly places, even as he chose us in him before the foundation of the world, that we should be holy and blameless before him." Before God ever created the world, he had a plan. He planned out the great story of redemption beforehand. Before the world was created, God sovereignly permitting and knowing that man would sin, chose to save a large remnant of humanity through His Son Jesus. And what we see in verse 4 is that

---

21 Thomas Watson, *The Doctrine of Repentance* (Edinburgh, UK: The Banner of Truth Trust, 2007), 45.

one of the purposes of saving His chosen people was to restore to them their lost holiness.

As human history began to unfold, we see this eternal purpose of God become evident. God says in Leviticus 11:45, "…I am the Lord who brought you up out of the land of Egypt to be your God. You shall therefore be holy, for I am holy." God saved His people, the Israelites, from slavery in Egypt, and in light of that salvation they were to live holy lives before the holy God. God's saving and delivering work was meant to lead them into greater love for God and obedience to His ways. One of the purposes of salvation was to restore them to holy living.

As the years went on, this truth did not change as God interacted with His people. Yet the nation of Israel constantly wandered from God and His holy ways. The people committed great idolatry against God and forsook His righteous laws. Over and over again, God describes His people as an unfaithful and adulterous wife. Though His people were unfaithful, God remained faithful to them and sought to restore them to Himself and His holiness.

We see this truth come out in the story of Hosea the prophet. God called Hosea to marry a prostitute in order to show symbolically God's faithful love for His unfaithful people. Though Hosea's wife continued in her unfaithfulness, the Lord said to Hosea, "'Go again, love a woman who is loved by another man and is an adulteress, even as the Lord loves the children of Israel, though they turn to other gods and love cakes of raisins.' So I bought her for fifteen shekels of silver and a homer and a lethech of barley. And I said to her, 'You must dwell as mine for many days. You shall not play the whore, or belong to another man; so will I also be to you.' For the children of Israel shall dwell many days without king or prince, without sacrifice or pillar, without ephod or household gods. Afterward the children of Israel shall return and seek the Lord their

God, and David their king, and they shall come in fear to the Lord and to his goodness in the latter days." (Hosea 3:1-5)

Hosea was to continue loving his unfaithful wife just as God continued to love his unfaithful wife, Israel. So we see that Hosea goes to her and redeems her, buying her out of her slavery to prostitution. But what we notice is that after freeing her from slavery to prostitution, he does not just let her go and be free to do whatever she wants. He commands and calls her to be completely faithful to him, just as he is faithful to her. In the same way, God redeems and buys His unfaithful people out of their slavery to sin, in order that they would walk in holiness and faithful love to Him.

What is clear from Scripture is that He has done this for us through His Son Jesus. First Peter 1:15 and 18-19 state, "…As he who called you is holy, you also must be holy in all your conduct, since it is written, 'You shall be holy, for I am holy' …knowing that you were ransomed from the futile ways inherited from your forefathers, not with perishable things such as silver or gold, but with the precious blood of Christ, like that of a lamb without blemish or spot."

God has ransomed and rescued us His people from slavery to our futile and selfish ways, not by silver or gold, but by the precious blood of Jesus. He has bought and brought us believers out of the darkness of our captivity to self-worship and self-seeking. Through the great price of His own life, Jesus has bought us, a people who were in bondage to sin, and has released us to live in the freedom and beauty of holiness before our great God. The purpose of the redeeming grace of Christ is to set us free to love and honor our holy God once again.

If you go to a wedding, it is likely you will see the bride wearing a white wedding dress. Ultimately, a white wedding dress is meant to be symbolic of the bride's purity. Ideally, a man wants to marry someone who is pure. The same is true in reference to Jesus. We as human beings were made for intimacy with God and God's Son. But for us to dwell in intimacy with God and come into His holy presence, we must be pure and holy as He is pure and holy. Jesus has bought and obtained a bride for Himself. But the bride He bought on the cross was an impure and unfaithful bride. For us impure and unfaithful people to be united in a marriage of eternal intimacy with Jesus, we must be made holy and pure.

The good news is, once we come to Jesus trusting Him for salvation, He cleanses us and begins purifying us to make us ready for the great day of our perfect marriage union with Him. Ephesians 5:25-27 states, "…Christ loved the church and gave himself up for her, that he might sanctify her, having cleansed her by the washing of water with the word, so that he might present the church to himself in splendor, without spot or wrinkle or any such thing, that she might be holy and without blemish." Jesus loved us in the midst of our filth and unfaithfulness and gave up His life to save us and bring us out of our sinful mess in order to present us as a holy, pure and faithful loving Bride before Him when He returns.

We must realize the great importance of personal holiness. God saved us for the purpose of restoring us to holiness. We cannot value its importance enough in our lives as Christians.

We Must Persevere in Holiness in Order to See the Lord

Fakes and imposters, who on the surface may seem inconspicuous, are somewhat easy to spot once you observe more closely. It is quite obvious that many men in our society are obsessed with following sports. I grew up playing sports, and I enjoy watching a game or two from time to time but when it comes down to it, I could care less. I no longer keep up with teams and players, so I do not really know what is going on in the world of sports today.

Sometimes I will find myself thrown into the middle of a sports conversation with other men, and though I do not have a clue what is going on, I try to talk the talk to the best of my ability. I know a little, but if you observe carefully, it is pretty evident that I am not a real sports fan.

The same is true when it comes to discerning true from fake Christians. In Matthew 7:15-20 Jesus states, "Beware of false prophets, who come to you in sheep's clothing but inwardly are ravenous wolves. You will recognize them by their fruits. Are grapes gathered from thorn bushes, or figs from thistles? So, every healthy tree bears good fruit, but the diseased tree bears bad fruit. A healthy tree cannot bear bad fruit, nor can a diseased tree bear good fruit. Every tree that does not bear good fruit is cut down and thrown into the fire. Thus you will recognize them by their fruits." Just as one is able to distinguish between a good and bad tree by observing its fruit, so can one distinguish between a true and false Christian by observing his or her actions.

It is clear from Scripture that those who are truly saved by God's grace will produce fruit of holiness throughout their lives. Holy living is the fruit, or evidence, that one has truly been born again into new life with God. If holiness is not there at all, then it proves that that person is not a true Christian. Our holiness does not save us. God's justifying grace which comes through faith in Jesus saves us. But the grace that justifies is the same grace that sanctifies. And if there is no sanctification then it proves there was no justification. Thus, holiness is essential and necessary if we are to be with the Lord in glory.

We see this in Scripture. Hebrews 12:14 says, "Strive...for holiness without which no one will see the Lord." Matthew 5:8 says, "Blessed are the pure in heart, for they shall see God." In Matthew 7:21 Jesus states, "Not everyone who says to me, 'Lord, Lord,' will enter the kingdom of heaven, but the one who does the will of my Father who is in heaven." The Lord warns us concerning the coming days of great evil: "the one who endures to the end will be saved" (Matt. 24:13).

Those who are walking in true holiness will be with the Lord. Those who are not walking in true holiness will not be with the Lord. First Corinthians 6:9-10 warns, "Do you not know that the unrighteous will not inherit the kingdom of God? Do not be deceived: neither the sexually immoral, nor idolaters, nor adulterers, nor men who practice homosexuality, nor thieves, nor the greedy, nor drunkards, nor revilers, nor swindlers will inherit the kingdom of God." Speaking of the New Jerusalem on the restored and glorified new earth, John says "…nothing unclean will ever enter it, nor anyone who does what is detestable or false…no longer will there be anything accursed" (Rev. 21:27; 22:3). Thus, we see the utmost importance of holiness in the Christian life.

God calls His people to persevere in bearing holy and good quality fruit. Second Peter 1:5-11 states, "For this very reason, make every effort to supplement your faith with virtue, and virtue with knowledge, and knowledge with self-control, and self-control with steadfastness, and steadfastness with godliness, and godliness with brotherly affection, and brotherly affection with love. For if these qualities are yours and are increasing, they keep you from being ineffective or unfruitful in the knowledge of our Lord Jesus Christ. For whoever lacks these qualities is so nearsighted that he is blind, having forgotten that he was cleansed from his former sins. Therefore, brothers, be all the more diligent to make your calling and election sure, for if you practice these qualities you will never fall. For in this way there will be richly provided for you an entrance into the eternal kingdom of our Lord and Savior Jesus Christ." Here we see a list of the holy and good quality fruits we are to be growing in as Christians. Our salvation by God's grace through faith in Christ is evidenced and shown to be sure as we grow in practicing and living out these qualities. And what we will have waiting for us in the end is entrance into the glorious kingdom of our great King Jesus.

Included within these qualities of the true Christian, Jesus gets more specific on the sort of fruit that is essential for the life of the Christian. In Matthew 25:31-46 Jesus speaks about the future judgment and the separation between the sheep and the goats, the true Christians and the non-Christians. Speaking to the sheep Jesus says, "Come, you who are blessed by my Father, inherit the kingdom prepared for you from the foundation of the world. For I was hungry and you gave me food, I was thirsty and you gave me drink, I was a stranger and you welcomed me, I was naked and you clothed me, I was sick and you visited me, I was in prison and you came to me" (Matt. 25:34-36). After asking Jesus when it was that they did these things for him, Jesus said, "Truly, I say to you, as you did it to one of the least of these my brothers, you did it to me" (Matt. 25:40). The same analysis takes place on the goats, and the lack of these qualities show that these are not the people of God. Therefore they are thrown into eternal punishment.

Taking care of the hungry, poor, needy and oppressed must be a fruit that is evident in the life of the true Christian. The total lack of this fruit shows that we never truly knew Christ. In order to stand before the Lord in glory, we must persevere in bearing these fruits of holiness.

The good news is that we do not have to struggle, strive, and seek to persevere in our own strength. We do not have to live in fear that we will be swallowed up and drawn away by the temptations of this world. First Thessalonians 5:23-24 states, "Now may the God of peace himself sanctify you completely, and may your whole spirit and soul and body be kept blameless at the coming of our Lord Jesus Christ. He who calls you is faithful; he will surely do it." As Christians, we cannot persevere in living lives of holiness in our own strength. Jude 24 says that God is the one who "…is able to keep you from stumbling and to present you blameless before the presence of his glory with great joy." By God's grace we are justified and by God's grace we are sanctified. Those who are true Christians do not have to lose heart because He will supply us with the grace and power we need to persevere in holy living. God is faithful not to leave us to our own strength but will finish the good work He started in us (Philippians 1:6).

As we have come to see the necessity and utmost importance of holiness for the life of a Christian, it is also important that we especially take heed to this in light of the coming days of increased lawlessness on the earth. The pursuit of holiness will be even more challenging as the days grow darker on the earth. Because of this, Jude gives us a charge that applies to his time, yet even more greatly to the times ahead. "But you must remember, beloved, the predictions of the apostles of our Lord Jesus Christ. They said to you, 'In the last time there will be scoffers, following their own ungodly passions.' It is these who cause divisions, worldly people, devoid of the Spirit. But you, beloved, build yourselves up in your most holy faith; pray in the Holy Spirit; keep yourselves in the love of God, waiting for the mercy of our Lord Jesus Christ that leads to eternal life" (Jude 17-21). In light of the times, may we all take heed to this great charge to persevere in the faith as we await the coming mercy of our Lord Jesus' appearing.

How to Grow in Holiness

We have been talking much about what holiness is and the great need for it in the life of the Christian. But the question now arises, how do we grow in holiness? Growing in holiness requires discipline, training and fighting that is empowered by the Holy Spirit. In order to grow in holiness we must have a wartime mindset. We must approach our pursuit of holiness as we would approach a war. This war is largely a war within (1 Pet. 2:11) and requires much training as we face the fight (1 Tim. 4:7).

The Word of God

For every battle you need a weapon. Our greatest and most important weapon in our battle for holiness is "the sword of the Spirit, which is the word of God" (Eph. 6:17). We must be disciplined and trained in using the sword of God's Word if we are to grow in holiness. This is the weapon the Spirit empowers us with to kill sin in our lives. Without it we will be defenseless and left defeated by our enemy, sin.

In Psalm 119 verses 9 and 11 say, "How can a young man keep his way pure? By guarding it according to your word ... I have stored up your word in my heart, that I might not sin against you." We guard our purity by holding up the shield of God's Word. We demolish sin in our lives by storing up the ammunition of God's Word in our hearts. It is through studying, memorizing, and meditating on the commands and promises of Scripture that we are enabled to grow in holiness before the Lord.

In Second Peter 1:4 we see that it is through God's "great promises" that we "may become partakers of the divine nature, having escaped from the corruption that is in the world because of sinful desire." In 2 Corinthians 7:1, after quoting a passage from Leviticus about the promise of God dwelling amongst His holy people, Paul writes, "Since we have these promises, beloved, let us cleanse ourselves from every defilement of body and spirit, bringing holiness to completion in the fear of God." By the promises of Scripture, we as Christians are enabled and motivated to turn from evil and walk in holy fear before the Lord.

Though all the commands, promises, and testimonies of Scripture are helpful in the fight for holiness, there are specific truths of Scripture that are essential meditations in the battle against sin. One very simple and important truth of Scripture that will help us in the fight is the truth of God's holiness. God says "You shall be holy, for I the Lord your God am holy" (Lev. 19:2). Meditating upon God's holiness will help us as His followers grow in holiness. Fixing your mind and heart upon the great perfection and purity of God as revealed in Scripture will motivate you as a Christian to be holy as God is holy. The more we focus on and realize the beauty of God's infinite purity and love, the more we will be inclined and drawn to pursue purity in our own lives.

Many times when people look at attractive people, they desire to become more attractive. As we look to the beautiful holiness of God, we should by His grace desire to be conformed more and more to the beauty of His holiness. Thus, meditating on Scriptures that speak of His holiness will be quite helpful in our personal pursuit of holy living.

The second very important and essential truth of God's Word to meditate upon in our struggle for holiness is the cross of our Lord Jesus. The nineteenth century Scottish pastor, Horatius Bonar, once wrote, "If we would be holy, we must get to the cross and dwell there."[22] To grow in holiness, we must meditate and dwell much upon that which is at the heart of Scripture, the cross of Jesus. The death of Jesus not only provided for us a right standing and a reconciled relationship with God, but also a new freedom and power to walk in holiness. Scripture teaches us that Christ's death for our sin also includes our death to sin. Romans 6:6-12 states, "We know that our old self was crucified with him in order that

---

22 Horatius Bonar, *God's Way of Holiness* (Scotland, UK: Christian Focus, 1999); as quoted in Joshua Harris, "Change Happens Because Of The Gospel," as cited on <http://www.joshharris.com/2006/10/change_happens_because_of_the.php; accessed 07 August 2009.

the body of sin might be brought to nothing, so that we would no longer be enslaved to sin. For one who has died has been set free from sin. Now if we have died with Christ, we believe that we will also live with him. We know that Christ being raised from the dead will never die again; death no longer has dominion over him. For the death he died he died to sin, once for all, but the life he lives he lives to God. So you also must consider yourselves dead to sin and alive to God in Christ Jesus. Let not sin therefore reign in your mortal bodies, to make you obey their passions."

At the cross, Jesus died to free us from the penalty of sin and the power of sin. When Jesus died on the cross, our sin died with Him. The dominion of our sin nature was nailed to the cross and drained of its power, thus releasing us from its captivity. Just as Christ died and rose again, we too have died to sin and are now alive to God. By faith in Him, we are now free and empowered to resist and to keep sin from dominating our lives.

For us as Christians to grow in holiness, we must study and meditate upon the redeeming power of the cross. The next time you are struggling with pride or selfishness, dwell upon the fact that Christ "gave himself for us to redeem us from all lawlessness and to purify for himself a people for his own possession who are zealous for good works" (Titus 2:14). The next time you are struggling with lust or anger, remember that the grace of God that has appeared bringing salvation is the same grace that is in the process of "training us to renounce ungodliness and worldly passions, and to live self-controlled, upright, and godly lives in the present age" (Titus 2:12). Think much and dwell much upon the transforming and liberating power of the cross as revealed in Scripture, that you may walk more and more in holiness.

The third essential and important truth of Scripture to meditate upon in our fight for holiness is heaven. We see this in Paul's prayer in Colossians 1:3-5: "We always thank God, the Father of our Lord Jesus Christ, when we pray for you, since we heard of your faith in Christ Jesus and of the love that you have for all the saints, because of the hope laid up for you in heaven." In Paul's prayer, we see that the Colossian believers' faith in Christ and love for the saints is based upon their hope in heaven. Their reason and motivation for having faith and love flow out of their future hope. As they fix their eyes on being with God in glory, they are enabled to exercise genuine faith in Christ and authentic love for the saints.

Being sober-minded, walking in purity, and putting to death sin, according to Scripture, comes about by fixing our minds and hearts upon the return of Jesus and our being with Him in glory. First Peter 1:13 says, "…preparing your minds for action, and being sober-minded, set your hope fully on the grace that will be brought to you at the revelation of Jesus Christ. First John 3:2-3 says, "Beloved, we are God's children now, and what we will be has not yet appeared; but we know that when he appears we shall be like him, because we shall see him as he is. And everyone who thus hopes in him purifies himself as he is pure." Colossians 3:1-5 exhorts, "If then you have been raised with Christ, seek the things that are above, where Christ is, seated at the right hand of God. Set your minds on things that are above, not on things that are on earth. For you have died, and your life is hidden with Christ in God. When Christ who is your life appears, then you also will appear with him in glory. Put to death therefore what is earthly in you: sexual immorality, impurity, passion, evil desire, and covetousness, which is idolatry."

We become sober-minded by setting our minds on the revelation of the returning Jesus. We purify ourselves by setting our minds on the hope that we will one day see Christ as He truly is in all His perfection and that we shall be like Him. We put to death what is earthly in us by focusing on heavenly things including the return of Jesus and being with Him in glory.

Heaven is a world of perfect holiness. The new heavens and the new earth that are coming will be a world of perfect love and never-ending joy. The more we meditate upon that world of perfect love and never-ending joy, the more we will begin to walk in that love and joy now. Looking to that world of holy love and joy is the driving force for holy living here and now. Studying and meditating on Scripture passages that speak of heaven will be key in your pursuit of holiness.

Thus we see that the Word of God is one of the mighty weapons of God essential in the battle for holiness. You must discipline and train yourself in the use of Scripture if you are going to be properly equipped for the battle. Every day is a battle to love the Lord and walk in holiness. Each new day we must reload and put the mighty words of God in our minds and hearts. Our minds must be covered and renewed by Scripture daily if we are going to have strength to gain new ground in the fight. Scripture study, memorization, and meditation must be continual in order for us to grow in holiness.

The Spirit of God

Though the Word of God is one of our great weapons and means by which we win the battle for holiness, by itself it is not enough. The Word of God is called "the sword of the Spirit," and is therefore the weapon the Spirit uses in believers to fight sin. But unless the hand and arm that swings the sword is strong and skillful, it does not matter how powerful the weapon itself is. The same is true with us as believers. If we pick up the sword of God's Word, but have no strength to swing it, we will have no victory in the fight for holiness.

That is where the Holy Spirit comes in. The Holy Spirit is the strength in our arms that helps us swing and chop off the ugly head of sin that appears in our lives. As we cling to the weapon of God's Word, our minds, hearts, and hands must be filled with the power of the Holy Spirit if we are going to effectively cut off the sin in our lives. John Owen writes of the Holy Spirit, "He only is sufficient for this work. All ways and means without him are as a thing of nought."[23]

This is clearly seen in Romans 8:12-13, where Paul writes, "... we are debtors, not to the flesh, to live according to the flesh. For if you live according to the flesh you will die, but if by the Spirit you put to death the deeds of the body, you will live." It is by the Holy Spirit that we as Christians are able to put to death sin in our lives. The power and grace that the Holy Spirit provides is the effective cause of all sin being put to death in our lives. Without His power, we are helpless. With His power, we can effectively demolish sin habits in our lives.

That is why we are commanded to "walk by the Spirit" (Gal. 5:16), meaning to walk in the desires and power of the Holy Spirit. If we walk by the Spirit, we "will not gratify the desires of the flesh" (Gal. 5:16).

But the question then becomes, how does the Holy Spirit unleash His power in our lives to kill sin? John Owen writes, "By causing our hearts to abound in grace, and the fruits that are contrary to the flesh and the fruits thereof, and to the principles of them. ... He causes us to grow, thrive, flourish and abound in those graces which are contrary, opposite, and destructive to all the fruits of the flesh, and to the quiet or thriving of indwelling sin itself."[24] In other words, instead of keeping us full with the rotten fruits of sin, He fills us with new grace to bear new and refreshing fruits that bring glory to God. "The fruit of the Spirit is love, joy, peace, patience, kindness, goodness, faithfulness, gentleness, self-control" (Gal. 5:22-23).

---

23 John Owen, *The Mortification of Sin* (Scotland: Christian Focus, 1996), 39.
24 Ibid, 44-45.

But what about us in this process? "If this be the work of the Spirit alone, how is it that we are exhorted to it?" writes Owen. The answer is that "He works upon our understandings, wills, consciences and affections, agreeably to their own natures: he works in us and with us, not against us or without us: so that his assistance is an encouragement as to the facilitating of the work, and no occasion of neglect as to the work itself."[25] Owen is saying that, yes it is true that it is by the power of the Holy Spirit alone that sin can be killed in our lives, but that does not leave us doing nothing. The Holy Spirit works in us, through us, and with us as we struggle, strive, read, pray and fight in His strength to kill sin in our lives. *We* must "put to death the deeds of the body." *We* must take action, but it is "by the Spirit," by His power that we can actually succeed in putting sin to death.

Prayer

To grow in holiness we must cling tightly to the Word of God and be empowered by the Holy Spirit. But there is a means by which we are empowered by the Holy Spirit and by which we rightly apply the Word of God in our fight with sin. That means is prayer. Just as a younger child who cannot reach something on a high shelf is prone to ask for help from their parents, we as children of God must be prone to ask our heavenly Father for help to reach the great heights of holiness that we cannot reach on our own. Jesus told us, "If you then, who are evil, know how to give good gifts to your children, how much more will the heavenly Father give the Holy Spirit to those who ask him!" (Luke 11:13).

If you want to grow in holiness, you must ask God for more of His Holy Spirit to fill you. You must ask that the Holy Spirit would fill you with more love, more joy, more purity and more faith. We see an example of this in Paul's prayer to the Ephesians

---

25 Ibid, 45-46.

in chapter three. He prays that the Father "may grant you to be strengthened with power through his Spirit in your inner being, so that Christ may dwell in your hearts through faith—that you, being rooted and grounded in love…" (Eph. 3:16-17). Here we see Paul praying for the power of the Holy Spirit to cause Christ to dwell in the Ephesian believers' hearts through faith and for them to be rooted and grounded in His immeasurable love. And in the same letter, in the context of fighting evil and the evil one, we are told that we need to be "praying at all times in the Spirit, with all prayer and supplication" (Eph. 6:18). Our fight for holiness, clinging to the weapon of God's Word, and being empowered by the Holy Spirit, all must be closely connected with prayer.

The importance of prayer in the fight for holiness is evident in other places in the New Testament. In Philippians 1:9-11 Paul states, "And it is my prayer that your love may abound more and more, with knowledge and all discernment, so that you may approve what is excellent, and so be pure and blameless for the day of Christ, filled with the fruit of righteousness that comes through Jesus Christ, to the glory and praise of God." In Colossians 1:10-12, Paul prays that the Colossian believers may "walk in a manner worthy of the Lord, fully pleasing to him, bearing fruit in every good work and increasing in the knowledge of God." He also prays, "may you be strengthened with all power, according to his glorious might, for all endurance and patience with joy, giving thanks to the Father, who has qualified you to share in the inheritance of the saints in light." Jesus Himself in the Lord's Prayer taught us to pray that the Father would "lead us not into temptation, but deliver us from evil" (Matt. 6:13). Thus, if we would grow in holiness, it is extremely important that we pray hard.

Holy Living Will Quicken the Return of the Lord Jesus

Thus far we have been talking about the utmost importance of holiness in the Christian life, what it consists of, and how we grow in it. But another crucial and amazing aspect of holiness that must be mentioned is that it literally quickens the return of Jesus to the earth. Deep holiness in the life of the church worldwide will help speed the return of Jesus. This is clearly seen in 2 Peter 3:10-13: "But the day of the Lord will come like a thief, and then the heavens will pass away with a roar, and the heavenly bodies will be burned up and dissolved, and the earth and the works that are done on it will be exposed. Since all these things are thus to be dissolved, what sort of people ought you to be in lives of holiness and godliness, waiting for and hastening the coming of the day of God, because of which the heavens will be set on fire and dissolved, and the heavenly bodies will melt as they burn! But according to his promise we are waiting for new heavens and a new earth in which righteousness dwells."

In light of the return of Jesus and the works of mankind being exposed before God, we as God's people ought to be living lives of holiness and godliness. And as we, the church, live holy and godly lives in anticipation of the coming new heavens and new earth, this somehow hastens, or quickens, the return of Jesus. It is clear from Scripture that God the Father will present a spotless Bride to His precious Son. In the final days, though many professed believers will fall away, the true church will arise in victory and flourish in purity in anticipation for the Bridegroom's return. Speaking of the marriage supper of the Lamb, Revelation 19:7-8 says, "'His (Jesus') Bride has made herself ready; it was granted her to clothe herself with fine linen, bright and pure'—for the fine linen is the righteous deeds of the saints." Before He returns, His Bride will be prepared, clothed in purity and righteousness.

In the end, though lawlessness will increase on the earth, the body of Christ will arise in triumph and will be walking in increased holiness (though not perfection). Are you walking in increasing holiness as you anticipate the return of Jesus? Are you helping speed the coming of Jesus by the purity of your life?

Warning: The Corruption of the Church

Though God's people are called to be holy, and while the true church will arise in victorious persevering holiness in the end, there is corruption within the church that we must consider, be warned of and turn from. The church has always dealt with false teaching and corruption of many kinds. We see this in the historic churches of the book of Revelation, specifically in the churches in Pergamum and Thyatira. The message to the church in Pergamum in Revelation 2:14 states, "But I have a few things against you: you have some there who hold the teaching of Balaam, who taught Balak to put a stumbling block before the sons of Israel, so that they might eat food sacrificed to idols and practice sexual immorality." The message to the church in Thyatira in Revelation 2:20-23 states, "But I have this against you, that you tolerate that woman Jezebel, who calls herself a prophetess and is teaching and seducing my servants to practice sexual immorality and to eat food sacrificed to idols. I gave her time to repent, but she refuses to repent of her sexual immorality. Behold, I will throw her onto a sickbed, and those who commit adultery with her I will throw into great tribulation, unless they repent of her works, and I will strike her children dead. And all the churches will know that I am he who searches mind and heart, and I will give to each of you as your works deserve."

These churches were being led astray by false teaching into immoral and idolatrous lifestyles. In Thyatira, we are told that they tolerated this false teaching and this promotion of immorality and idolatry. Many within the church did not take a stand against it.

In fact, this is what we see in many American churches today. The Western church largely tolerates the idolatry of money and the perversion of sexuality in our culture. The pursuit of holiness and the fight for purity is lacking in many churches today. On a large scale, the church is laced with worldliness and tainted with the consumerism and lust of our age. Jesus warns the Western church, just as He warned the church in Thyatira, that we must repent or else suffer judgment.

As the days grow darker, as lawlessness increases on the earth, we must especially be warned of the corruption that can easily overtake the church. Speaking of the coming one world political, economic, and religious system of Babylon, Revelation 18:2-5 states, "She has become a dwelling place for demons, a haunt for every unclean spirit, a haunt for every unclean bird, a haunt for every unclean and detestable beast. For all nations have drunk the wine of the passion of her sexual immorality, and the kings of the earth have committed immorality with her, and the merchants of the earth have grown rich from the power of her luxurious living….Come out of her, my people, lest you take part in her sins, lest you share in her plagues; for her sins are heaped high as heaven, and God has remembered her iniquities."

God is warning the church that the days are evil, and days of increased wickedness are coming. By His grace we must pursue holiness and come out from the impurities and corruption of this world. If we do not, we will have a share in the plagues of God's judgment and thus prove we were never His children. God calls His church to persevere in holiness to the very end as we anticipate the day Jesus returns and banishes sin from our lives for good.

CHAPTER 4

The Time is Short— Use it Well

The clock ticks. Second by second, hour by hour, day by day, the clock ticks away. Each breath breathed and each moment spent passes and cannot be regained. For all of us, time moves forward and quite quickly it seems. We look back five or ten years ago and it seems like just yesterday. We are locked in time knowing it will one day run out, just like a prisoner on death row who sits in his cell awaiting his execution. Thinking of the fleeting of time can be depressing and quite sobering, and yet it can spur us on to use our time well, especially in the light of Jesus' Second Coming.

In the 1989 movie *Dead Poets Society*, Robin Williams plays the part of John Keating, an unconventional English teacher at a prep school for boys. He teaches outside of the box and dares his students to dream big. At one point in the movie, he calls on one of his students to read the first stanza of a poem entitled, "*To Virgins, To Make Much of Time*." The student reads, "Gather ye rosebuds while ye may, Old Time is still a-flying; and this same flower that smiles today, To-morrow will be dying."

Williams responds, "The Latin term for that sentiment is *carpe diem*. Who knows what that means?" One of the students responds, "*Carpe Diem*, that's 'seize the day.'" Williams responds, "Very good…. 'Seize the day.' 'Gather ye rosebuds while ye may.'

Why does the writer use these lines?" One student responds, "Because he's in a hurry." The students laugh. Williams responds, "No, ding! Thank you for playing anyway....Because we are food for worms, lads. Because, believe it or not, each and every one of us in this room is one day going to stop breathing, turn cold, and die." As he has the students look at some pictures of students from a previous generation, he says, "They believe they are destined for great things just like many of you are. Their eyes are full of hope just like you. Did they wait till it was too late to make from their lives even one iota of what they were capable? Because you see, gentlemen, these boys are now fertilizing daffodils. But if you listen real close, you can hear them whisper their legacy to you.... Go ahead, lean in, listen. Do you hear it? '*Carpe. Carpe. Carpe diem*. Seize the day, boys. Make your lives extraordinary.'"[26]

The Fleeting of Time and the Uncertainty of Life

In this scene of the movie, we are forced to face the fleeting of time, the uncertainty of tomorrow and the certainty of future death. The Scriptures also point out this reality we must face: "All flesh is grass, and all its beauty is like the flower of the field. The grass withers, the flower fades when the breath of the Lord blows on it; surely the people are grass" (Isa. 40-6-7). "The years of our life are seventy, or even by reason of strength eighty; yet their span is but toil and trouble; they are soon gone, and we fly away" (Ps. 90:10).

Though we might live to old age, we cannot automatically assume that we will. "Come now, you who say, 'Today or tomorrow we will go into such and such a town and spend a year there and trade and make a profit'—yet you do not know what tomorrow will bring. What is your life? For you are mist that appears for a little time and then vanishes" (James 4:13-14). Our time is short.

---

26 *Dead Poets Society*, dir. Peter Weir with performance by Robin Williams (Hollywood: Touchstone Pictures, 1989), feature film.

How should we respond to this sobering reality? By saying with the psalmist, "Teach us to number our days that we may get a heart of wisdom" (Ps. 90:12). We must first realize and soak into our hearts the preciousness of time and, from that place of understanding, live wisely.

Redeem the Time

When we face the stark reality that our life is but a vapor, we can then be in a position to live intentionally and use our time well to the glory of God. As John Keating (Robin Williams), spoke to his students about the fleetingness of life, he used that as a springboard to challenge them to seize the day and make their lives extraordinary. As Christians, we are called to seize each day, redeem each day, each moment even, and use it for the glory of God. Speaking of how we use our days R.C. Sproul writes, "We all have an equal measure of time in every day. Where we differ from one another is in how we redeem the time allotted. When something is redeemed it is rescued or purchased from some negative condition. The basic negative condition we are concerned with is the condition of waste. To waste time is to spend it on that which has little or no value."[27]

To redeem time is to rescue it from the waste can of unwise living and bring it into the place of good God-glorifying use. Ephesians 5:15-16 tells us, "Look carefully then how you walk, not as unwise but as wise, making the best use of the time, because the days are evil." If we are going to use our time on earth wisely and put it to its best use, there are two things we must do. First, we must observe carefully how we are using our time already and see how we can use it more wisely. We need to repent of our bad use of time and then learn how to put it to good use. Second, realizing that the

27 R.C. Sproul, "Time Well Spent," (Tabletalk, September 1997); as quoted in C.J. Mahaney, "Biblical Productivity," as cited on http://www.sovereigngraceministries.org/Reference/Blog/cj-mahaney-biblical-productivity.pdf; accessed 27 April 2009.

days are evil can help us put our time to better use. Paul was living in evil days; we are living in even more evil days. And as the days go on and we get closer to the return of Christ, they will get increasingly evil. Living in these dark days should wake us up to the serious reality that time is short, God's judgment is coming upon this wicked planet, and we are to be looking forward to Christ's eternal kingdom of righteousness that is to come. We must make the most of every opportunity because how we live in these evil days will determine what kind of impact we make for eternity.

Bad Use of Time

If we are going to make the best use of our time on earth, we must know the difference between unworthy and worthy pursuits. What would be considered a bad and unworthy use of our time? What would be considered a good and worthy use of our time? Ultimately, bad use of time can be summed up in what could be called our love affair with the world. Another term for this is "worldliness." Like a young couple who are madly in love with each other, we are stuck on and obsessed with the ways of this world. This should not be the case for us as Christians.

First John 2:15-17 states, "Do not love the world or the things in the world. If anyone loves the world, the love of the Father is not in him. For all that is in the world—the desires of the flesh and the desires of the eyes and pride in possessions—is not from the Father but is from the world. And the world is passing away along with its desires, but whoever does the will of God abides forever." Loving the world is a waste of time for several reasons. First, God commands us not to love the world. We would do well to listen to our Creator. Second, those who love the world prove that they do not really know and love God. Third, the world with its desires is passing away. It makes no sense to put all of one's energy and hope in something that will pass away. Thus, it is clear that to love the world is to waste one's precious time.

But we must ask, what does it mean to love the world? If we want to avoid this meaningless love affair with the world, we need to know what love for the world means exactly. Loving the world, in this context, has nothing to do with loving the created world but instead refers to having a love for the ways of this corrupted age. The ways of this world that we are to turn from consist of the desires of the flesh, the desires of the eyes, and the pride in possessions (or "pride of life").

Let's start with the desires of the flesh. What does this refer to? Matthew Henry, in his commentary, writes, "*The flesh* here, being distinguished from *the eyes* and *the life,* imports the body. The lust of the flesh is, subjectively, the humour and appetite of indulging fleshly pleasures..."[28] In other words, the desires of the flesh refer to the cravings of the body to indulge in sinful pleasures. The desires of the flesh would refer to sexual impurity, drunkenness, outbursts of anger, inappropriate use of words such as coarse joking, addictions to food, coffee, etc., and the list could go on. To live consumed with the desires of the flesh is to walk in love with the world and out of love with God, which results in wasted time.

Next we see desires of the eyes mentioned. The desires of the eyes seems to refer to what we are told not to do in the tenth commandment, "You shall not covet." To covet is to see something and want something that is not yours in such an overwhelming and disproportionate way that you would be discontent without it. In Scripture, covetousness equals idolatry (Col. 3:5). In the Old Testament, we see the Israelites constantly turning from God to make visible tangible gods of their own that they followed. We do the same thing. We look upon the created things and people of

28 Matthew Henry, *Matthew Henry's Commentary on the Whole Bible* (New York: Fleming H. Revell Company), 6:1069.

this world in order to find ultimate hope and satisfaction, and in doing so, exchange the glory of God for these idols of our covetous hearts (Rom. 1:23, 25). Following the desires of wandering worldly eyes leads us away from the one life-giving God who is truly worth our time and worship.

Lastly, we see pride in possessions mentioned or "pride of life" as some translations render it. To love the world is to love the honor, praise, position and wealth that this world can offer. To put all your stock in wealth and status, comfort and security, is to be drawn into the alluring pride of possessions. Boasting in what one has achieved and acquired is the essence of this pride in possessions, and it is a deadly waste of time. "They… whose time is taken up in caring and labouring for the world only, in inquiring what they shall eat, and what they shall drink, and wherewithal they shall be clothed; in contriving to lay up for themselves treasures upon earth, how to enrich themselves, how to make themselves great in the world, or how to live in comfortable and pleasant circumstances, while here; who busy their minds and employ their strength in these things only, and the stream of whose affections is directed towards these things; they lose their precious time."[29]

Putting your confidence, trust and hope in things will leave you nowhere but in a place of danger. Jesus once told a parable to help us understand this: "The land of a rich man produced plentifully, and he thought to himself, 'What shall I do, for I have nowhere to store my crops?' And he said, 'I will do this: I will tear down my barns and build larger ones, and there I will store all my grain and my goods. And I will say to my soul, Soul, you have ample goods laid up for many years; relax, eat, drink, be merry.' But God said to him, 'Fool! This night your soul is required of you, and the things you have prepared, whose will they be?' So

29 Jonathan Edwards, *The Works of Jonathan Edwards* (Peabody, MA: Hendrickson Publishers, Inc., September 2005), 2:235.

is the one who lays up treasure for himself and is not rich toward God" (Luke 12:16-21).

Storing up and trusting in wealth and earthly comfort is a waste of time because it will have no value when one faces God on the Day of Judgment. Proverbs 11:4, 7, and 28 show us exactly where pride in possessions will lead us: "Riches do not profit in the day of wrath....When the wicked dies, his hope will perish, and the expectation of wealth perishes too....Whoever trusts in riches will fall."

We as American Christians need to wake up and see just how prideful and idolatrous we really are in regards to wealth, security and leisure. The sad truth is, "We have become ensnared by un-precedented material luxury. Advertising constantly convinces us that we need one unnecessary luxury after another. Affluence is the god of 20th century [21st as well, my addition] North Americans...We are caught in an absurd, materialistic spiral. The more we make, the more we think we need in order to live decently and respectably."[30]

God is angry at the materialism and idolatry of comfort that pervades our culture. How dare we, as His blood-bought people, fall in line with secular society and replace the one true God with the false gods of materialism and comfort? Just as Israel forgot the Lord and went after the idols of the surrounding culture, we have forgotten God and have gone after the idols of our secular culture. In Deuteronomy 8, God warned His people not to forget Him once they were brought into the land of prosperity. If they did forget Him, they would be judged.

In Amos 6 we also see God warning His people that judg-ment would come because of their idolatry of wealth, security, and leisure. "Woe to those who are at ease in Zion, and to those

30 Ron Sider, *Rich Christians in an Age of Hunger: Moving From Affluence to Gener-osity* (W Publishing Group, 1997), 191-192.

who feel secure on the mountain of Samaria...Woe to those who lie on beds of ivory and stretch themselves out on their couches, and eat lambs from the flock and calves from the midst of the stall, who sing idle songs to the sound of the harp and like David invent for themselves instruments of music, who drink wine in bowls and anoint themselves with the finest oils, but are not grieved over the ruin of Joseph! Therefore they shall now be the first of those who go into exile, and the revelry of those who stretch themselves out shall pass away" (Amos 6:1, 4-7).

Does this condition not sound like the American church? Woe to us! We must repent and turn to the cross of Jesus. Seeking constant luxury and leisure has become ingrained within our way of life. Many of us may not even realize it. Yet it is true. Convenience and ease have become our day-to-day goals. Entertainment and fun have become our most prized possessions and what we look forward to most in any given week. This is heinous. We would rather watch a movie or a sports game than fellowship with the triune God. We are more entertained by TV than by the almighty God of the universe. Oh, how perverse have we become? We are wasting our lives. We were made for so much more.

John Piper, reflecting on similar thoughts, writes, "At these moments, when the trifling fog of life clears and I see what I am on earth to do, I groan over the petty pursuits that waste so many lives—and so much of mine. Just think of the magnitude of sports—a whole section of the daily newspaper. But there is no section on God. Think of the endless resources for making your home and garden more comfortable and impressive. Think of how many tens of thousands of dollars you can spend to buy more car than you need. Think of the time and energy and conversation that go into entertainment and leisure and what we call 'fun stuff.' And add to that now the computer that artificially recreates the very games that are already so distant from reality; it is like a multi-layered dreamworld of insignificance expanding into nothingness. Or think about clothes. What a tragedy to see so many young people obsessed with what they wear and how they look."[31]

This is what wasted time and a wasted life looks like. Loving the ways of the world, following the desires of the flesh, the desires of the eyes, and the pride in possessions result in precious time wasted and eternal significance lost. Time is short. The days are evil. Do not waste it by being sucked into a deceptive and destructive love affair with this decaying world.

Break the Attachment—Look to Eternity

The danger of wasting time for many Christians is not simply found in following the sinful patterns of the world but rather in being stuck in the rut of day-to-day living with no view of eternity. Being fixated and consumed with our day-to-day relationships and tasks can cause us to take our eyes off eternity. We are creatures of habit who like familiarity. This is not necessarily a bad thing, but it can be. We are prone to be attached to certain relationships and certain interactions we have in the world in a way that takes our gaze off of Christ's eternal kingdom.

Thus Paul gives us a highly relevant warning and exhortation: "…The appointed time has grown very short. From now on, let those who have wives live as though they had none, and those who mourn as though they were not mourning, and those who rejoice as though they were not rejoicing, and those who buy as though they had no goods, and those who deal with the world as though they had no dealings with it. For the present form of this world is passing away" (1 Cor. 7:29-31). What does this mean? It does not mean that everything in this world is evil. Marriage is a gift from God. Material possessions can be helpful to have. Work-

---

31 John Piper, *Don't Waste Your Life*, 125.

ing and taking care of day-to-day affairs are good and respectable pursuits. What then, does this mean?

What Paul is saying to us is that though we use the world and interact in the world, we are not to hold on to it too tightly. We are not to become attached and fixated to the present form of this world. Though we are called to invest our emotions, thoughts and energy into our relationships and interactions with the world, we must not do so in such a way as though we were seeking ultimate comfort, meaning and satisfaction in this world. Though we mourn over our losses and trials, we do not despair. We look for the day when God will wipe away all our tears and pain. Though we rejoice in our earthly joys, we do not put all our joy in the present form of this world. We look forward to new heavens and a new earth where we will dwell in fullness of joy forever.

The appointed time has grown very short. The present form of this world is passing away. It would be foolish to live for the shadows when we await the substance. Let us not waste our time by being attached to the world as it is, but let us live our day-to-day lives with eternity in view as we await the coming new heavens and new earth.

Good Use of Time

So far we have looked at those bad uses of time, and now we turn to look at what would be good uses of our time. To know what a good use of our time is, we need to ask two main questions. First, how will this glorify God and exalt Christ? Second, how will this impact eternity?

In Scripture we find several things that are important for us to pursue in order to bring glory to God and make an impact for eternity. I will list some of those main things that are of the utmost importance (this is not an exhaustive list):

1. Pursue Intimacy with God. The first commandment is love God with all your heart, soul, mind, and strength. This is the reason we were created—to love God. If we are going to glorify God and prepare for eternity, we must pursue intimacy with Him. This means we must study the revelation of His heart and will. We must study the Bible. We must learn to commune with Him in prayer and hunger for Him through fasting. We must learn what it means to walk in daily worship of Him, exalting Him for all that He is and all that He has done for us through Jesus, our precious Savior.

2. Pursue holiness. "Strive for holiness...without which no one will see the Lord" (Heb. 12:14). Holiness is essential for the Christian life. In order to be with the Lord in glory, we must persevere by His grace in holy living. Heaven will be a holy place of holy love. If we are going to prepare for eternity, we must pursue holiness now.

3. Pray (Intercede). As Christians, we are called to "pray without ceasing." One can never pray enough. One can never stress the importance of prayer too much. Prayer is powerful. "The prayer of a righteous person has great power as it is working" (James 5:16). We are called to pray for the people of God, the lost, the oppressed, and the unreached peoples of the world. If we are abiding in Christ and in His Word (John 15:7), our prayers will have great effectiveness and impact on eternity beyond what we can imagine or accomplish through our own actions. Martyn Lloyd-Jones once wrote, "Go on with all your activities, if you wish to do so. Go on with your work. I am not saying that you should stop all your efforts and just wait. No, go on, if you like, doing all that you are doing, but I do say this— make certain that you leave time to pray for revival, and to see that that has more time than anything else. Because when the Holy Ghost comes in power, more will happen in an hour than will happen in fifty or even a hundred years as a result of your exertions and mine."[32]

4. Maintain Fellowship with Christians. Be committed to a local church. We need each other. We need the local church. If we are going to persevere in the faith till the end and make a great impact for eternity, we must stick together and be committed to a local body of believers. We will be worshiping our triune God forever together. We need to prepare for that reality here and now.

5. Proclaim the Gospel and Make Disciples. Jesus told us to go and make disciples. Every day we meet people who are on their way to eternal punishment in hell. One of the greatest impacts we can make for eternity is to share the good news of Jesus Christ with lost people on a regular basis. But there is a need for so much more. For people to be prepared for eternity, they need more than just forgiveness. Christ calls us to not just make converts but to make disciples, radical followers of Him. Our goal should be Paul's goal, "Him we proclaim, warning everyone and teaching everyone with all wisdom, that we may present everyone mature in Christ" (Col. 1:28). We are called to invest in believers that they may be built up into mature followers of Christ. Just think of the eternal impact we could make if we took the time to do this.

6. Go to the Nations. Not only are we told to go and make disciples but we are told to go to "all nations" and make disciples. There are billions of unreached people in the world today. We live in a country that has had access to the gospel for a long time. And yet there are millions who have never even heard the name of Jesus. Oh, how worthy an investment of your time it would be to go to a place that has never heard the name of Christ! That would be time well spent!

---

32 Martyn Lloyd-Jones, *Revival* (Wheaton, IL: Crossway Books, 1987), 210. Used by permission of Crossway, a publishing ministry of Good News Publishers, Wheaton, IL 60187, www.crossway.org.

7. Serve the Poor and Oppressed. The Scripture is filled with commands to help the poor and oppressed of society. James tells us that our religion is impure and defiled if we do not help the helpless (James 1:27). Jesus seemed to think it was a pretty big deal. So much so that not helping the poor and oppressed results in eternal hell (Matt. 25:41-46). Think of the billions that go hungry every day. Think of the countless orphans. Think of the millions of women and children who have been forced into sexual slavery. As Christ's followers, we are called to "seek justice and correct oppression" (Isa. 1:17) that "they may see (our) good works and give glory to (our) Father who is heaven" (Matt. 5:16).

8. Rest and, with Balance, Enjoy God's Good Creation. We are to "remember the Sabbath day, to keep it holy" (Ex. 19:8). God calls his people to rest. Sunday is now the Christian's Sabbath. We are to rest, celebrate, and worship on this great day of the week just as the early church did (Acts 20:7, 1 Cor. 16:1-2). Though we are called to work hard for the Lord, doing His will with the short time we have on this earth, we must remember to rest. God commands us to rest and He is glorified in this. God calls us to enjoy His good creation unto His glory. "Whether you eat or drink, or whatever you do, do all to the glory of God" (1 Cor. 10:31). We can rest, play, and enjoy good times with friends and family, unto the glory of God. And yet, as I mentioned, we are to enjoy God's good creation "with balance." As we take time to rest and enjoy creation here and now, we must not become slothful and idolatrous. We look forward to a greater place of rest that Christ will usher in when He comes again.

9. Use the specific gifts God has given you. This is important. Up until now I have simply been mentioning those things in which all Christians should be investing their time in order to make an eternal impact for the glory of God. But something else we must consider is that God has given us all different gifts and means to accomplish those realities. Jesus tells us a very important parable that we need to consider. Matt. 25:14-30 says,

"For it will be like a man going on a journey, who called his servants and entrusted to them his property. To one he gave five talents, to another two, to another one, to each according to his ability. Then he went away. He who had received the five talents went at once and traded with them, and he made five talents more. So also he who had the two talents made two talents more. But he who had received the one talent went and dug in the ground and hid his master's money. Now after a long time the master of those servants came and settled accounts with them. And he who had received the five talents came forward, bringing five talents more, saying, 'Master, you delivered to me five talents; here I have made five talents more.' His master said to him, 'Well done, good and faithful servant. You have been faithful over a little; I will set you over much. Enter into the joy of your master.' And he also who had the two talents came forward, saying, 'Master, you delivered to me two talents; here I have made two talents more.' His master said to him, 'Well done, good and faithful servant. You have been faithful over a little; I will set you over much. Enter into the joy of your master.' He also who had received the one talent came forward, saying, 'Master, I knew you to be a hard man, reaping where you did not sow, and gathering where you scattered no seed, so I was afraid, and I went and hid your talent in the ground. Here you have what is yours.' But his master answered him, 'You wicked and slothful servant! You knew that I reap where I have not sown and gather where I scattered no seed? Then you ought to have invested my money with the bankers, and at my coming I should have received what was my own with interest. So take the talent from him and give it to him who has the ten talents. For to everyone who has will more be given, and he will have an abundance. But from the one who has not, even what he has will be taken away. And cast the worthless servant into the outer darkness. In that place there will be weeping and gnashing of teeth.'"

Here we see this master entrusting to his servants different amounts of money. Five talents to one, two talents to another, and one talent to yet another. Each was expected to use well what he was given. The one with five talents produced five more and was commended by the master. The one with two talents produced two more and was also commended. And yet the one with one talent did not produce anything more and was punished severely for his negligence.

In the same way, God has given all Christians gifts to be used well for His glory and the spread of His kingdom. He has given each one of us certain spiritual and natural gifts. He has endowed each of us with certain financial blessings. He has placed certain vocational callings upon our lives. He has allotted to each one of us a certain amount of time on earth to do His will and use well what has been given to us. What are your spiritual gifts (Rom. 12:6-8; 1 Cor. 12:1-11; Eph. 4:11)? What natural gifts and personality traits has God given you to be used for His glory? What vocational callings has he placed upon your life? What finances has He blessed you with for the spread of His gospel? What desires and burdens has He laid on your heart for you to pursue for His purposes? What has God entrusted you with? This is important to understand because if you want to make maximum eternal impact with your life, you must not only follow the general commands of Scripture, but you must use well the gifts He has entrusted to you with the short amount of time He has given you.

In thinking about how to use our gifts well with the time we have been given, we must remember the serious reality of our accountability before God. Jonathan Edwards writes: "Time is a talent given us by God; he hath set us our day; and it is not for nothing, our day was appointed for some work; therefore he will, at the day's end, call us to an account. We must give account to him of the improvement of all our time. We are God's servants; as a servant is accountable to his master, how he spends his time when he is sent forth to work, so are we accountable to God. If men would aright consider this, and keep it in mind, would they not improve their time otherwise than they consider with yourselves every morning, that you must give an account to God, how you shall have spent that day? and if you considered with yourselves, at the beginning of every evening, that you must give an account to God, how you shall have spent that evening? Christ hath told us, that "for every idle word which men speak, they shall give account in the day of judgment," Matt. 12:36. How well, therefore, may we conclude, that we must give an account of all our idle misspent time!"[33]

Let us consider the seriousness of our accountability before God and seek to use our gifts and time well, that we may one day hear those lovely words: "Well done, good and faithful servant.... Enter into the joy of your master" (Matt. 25:11).

Practical Steps

Our time is precious and we want to use it well for God's glory, so we have looked at those general and most important Scriptural commands that we are to pursue wholeheartedly. We have also seen the importance of identifying the specific gifts and abilities God has entrusted to us. But at this point we must get more specific. How do we rightly apply and put into action these most worthy pursuits of our time? We must get down into the highly complex details of life in order to begin using our time well as we press forward to our end destination of glory.

---

33 Edwards, *The Works of Jonathan Edwards*, 2:235.

It is similar to viewing an online map. We look at the enlarged map and we see where we need to go, along with the main roads that will take us to our destination. But in order to arrive there most effectively, we must zoom in and get a glimpse of the more detailed roads and turns we will need to take. So it is in the Christian life. We know where we are headed and we know the main roads that we need to spend our time on as we approach our destination. But we also realize that those detailed and intricate turns are important as well. To use our time well on our way to our destination, we must follow the general paths of Scripture, as well as those more specific paths of gifting, roles, and planning. And just as it is important to stop and ask directions when there is a lack of clarity, we also must ask God for wisdom and direction on how to use our time most wisely along the way to glory.

As we have identified those most worthy pursuits of our time as revealed in Scripture and as identified in our gifts, we must now put these into action in the details of everyday life. We must learn how to channel these things rightly. So how do we do this?

First, we must identify our specific roles in life. Examples of roles would be as follows: Christian, single person, husband, wife, parent, employee, church leader, church member, etc. Discern what your roles are in life. Then ask the following questions: How can I apply the commands and teachings of Scripture to the context that I am in? How can I use well the gifts, finances, and traits God has given me in these contexts?

Second, pray for God's wisdom and direction. "If any of you lacks wisdom, let him ask God, who gives generously to all without reproach, and it will be given him" (James 1:5). We need God's help discerning how to apply the Scriptures and our particular gifts into the roles and context God has placed us in. For example, God calls us to disciple other believers.

Who are those people in your life that you need to invest in and what would be the best way of going about it? Maybe your spiritual gift is serving. What are the best ways to serve within your local church and community? Perhaps you are naturally gifted in working with your hands. What sort of job would be best to take in order to utilize that gift? What do your finances look like? How and where can you invest your money for the spread of the gospel? Consider these things and take them to God in prayer.

Third, we need to thoroughly think, plan and schedule the use of our time accordingly. Once we have identified those most worthy pursuits of our time and how they relate to our specific roles, we must be intentional and make plans concerning how to put these realities into action. Too much of the time we just let life flow and we respond to what comes our way. Do not get me wrong. Unexpected things happen and will happen. We must at times be flexible. But if we are going to make the best use of our time and gifts, we must learn to schedule and plan ways of putting these things to use. We must learn to live, not accidently, but intentionally. God calls us not to live carelessly but to "look carefully…how (we) walk" (Eph. 5:15).

Fourth, put your plan into action. Thorough thinking, praying, and planning must lead to action. We must step out and be obedient to God's Word and God's call on our lives. There will be times when we are unsure about the specifics of our callings and gifting. At those times we must continue to walk in those realities that are clearly revealed in Scripture. And as we seek Him, in time He will show us the particulars. Many times we will be called to take godly risks for the spread of the gospel of Christ and for the glory of His name. Are you stepping forward to put your time to good use for His kingdom?

Jesus is Coming Soon to Evaluate How You Spent Your Time on Earth

If you knew Jesus were to come back tomorrow, or next week, or even in a few short years, how would you be spending your time? The truth is, He is coming back soon. Scripture tells us this: "...And the Lord, the God of the spirits of the prophets, has sent his angel to show his servants what must *soon* take place...Behold, I am coming *soon*...the time is *near*...Behold, I am coming *soon*, bringing my recompense with me...Surely I am coming soon" (Rev. 22:6-7, 10, 12, 20, emphasis mine). The nearness of Jesus' Second Coming is emphasized five times in this chapter alone. This shows us how serious and important the matter is. What does this mean? These verses were written almost two thousand years ago. His Second Coming does not seem so soon compared to when this was written.

I believe the point of this emphasis is to stress to all believers of all times that we are to live with urgency. We are to live with urgency and we are to live consciously. We must continually be conscious of the fact that He is coming, "bringing (His) recompense with (Him), to repay everyone for what he has done" (Rev. 22:12). We are to be mindful of His coming evaluation of our lives. He is coming to evaluate how we spent our time and how we used the life God graciously gave us. Are you living with urgency, conscious of His imminent return?

Though I believe these warnings of the nearness of His coming are meant to cause all believers to live with urgency, there is a sense in which these warnings will have greater urgency as the time gets nearer to His coming. In fact, Jesus told us the things that would be happening before he returned (Matt. 24) and that that generation would "know that he is near" (Matt. 24:33) when they see these realities unfold. When these things begin to happen, we will feel the weight and intensity of these warnings of His imminent return even more. I believe that hour is fast approaching.

An Exhortation to Work Hard for the Lord as the Day Draws Nearer

Paul commands us, "Do not be slothful in zeal, be fervent in spirit, serve the Lord" (Rom. 12:11). As you seek to use your short amount of time well, take heed to these words. In all your studying, in all your praying, in all your obedience, in all your work, in all your resting, in all your faithful service, do not be lazy in your passion for God, but be consumed with a fervent desire for Christ's glory to spread. Serve the Lord with fullness of heart, mind, soul, and strength. Strive to work for the Lord in such a way that you can say with the Apostle Paul, "I worked harder than any of them though it was not I, but the grace of God that is with me" (1 Cor. 15:10). One day very soon Christ will raise us up and we will all be changed, forever with Him in glory. "Therefore, my beloved brothers, be steadfast, immovable, always abounding in the work of the Lord, knowing that in the Lord your labor is not in vain" (1 Cor. 15:58).

CHAPTER 5

Prepare to Suffer

All good stories have a happy ending. God's redemptive story seen throughout history will have the happiest of all endings, when Christ comes back to fully establish His kingdom of glory and love. But just because all good stories have a happy ending does not mean there are no tragedies and trials within. All good stories have an element of tension, struggle, or loss. It is no less the case in the true story of God's redemption.

Ever since the fall of man, suffering has been a part of this world and a part of the lives of every human being who has ever walked the planet. Death and suffering have entered our world as a result of our rebellion against God. Though this is true, God has redemptive purposes in suffering. In His divine wisdom, God takes what is bad and harmful, turns it around, and orchestrates it for good. This is most supremely evident in the gruesome death of the Son of God, who by His death swallowed up God's righteous wrath towards sin, thus providing salvation for the nations.

As seen in the death of Christ, suffering can have a redemptive quality to it. Though only Christ's sufferings have the power to save; good purposes can come about through our suffering as well. That is why it should not shock us that God has called all Christians to suffer. Though we are not to seek out suffering, following Christ means we must be willing and ready to suffer. To follow Christ means we will have to face suffering. We will not escape the pains that this world faces everyday. In fact, as Christians we will be called to suffer in unique ways that go above and beyond the normal trials of everyday life.

The clear call of the Christian to suffer is evident throughout the New Testament. "And he [Jesus] said to all, 'If anyone would come after me, let him deny himself and take up his cross daily and follow me…' (Luke 9:23). "In the world you will have tribulation" (John 16:33). "Through many tribulations we must enter the kingdom of God" (Acts 14:22). "For it has been granted to you that for the sake of Christ you should not only believe in him but also suffer for his sake" (Philippians 1:29).

In light of the clear teaching of Scripture, we should not be surprised when we go through trials and are called to suffer for the sake of His kingdom. And yet, this seems to be the case for most Western Christians. We are caught off guard when suffering comes and we do not know how to respond. Commenting on this problem Ajith Fernando, youth director for Youth for Christ in Sri Lanka, writes, "I think one of the most serious theological blind spots in the Western church is a defective understanding of suffering. There seems to be a lot of reflection on how to avoid suffering and on what to do when we hurt. We have a lot of teaching about escape from and therapy for suffering, but there is inadequate teaching about the theology of suffering. Christians are not taught why they should expect suffering as followers of Christ and why suffering is so important for healthy growth as a Christian."[34]

This is a serious problem because without this clear understanding of the role of suffering in the life of a Christian, we will be deficient in our ability to handle and respond to suffering

---

34 Ajith Fernando, *The Call to Joy and Pain: Embracing Suffering in Your Ministry* (Wheaton, IL: Crossway Books, 2007), 51-52.

in a God-glorifying way when it comes. Therefore, "...we must prepare, because the ideal time to be educated about suffering is never in the midst of it. We need to be trained prior to suffering, so that we may be fully sustained in suffering."[35] The Western church desperately needs to learn how to be prepared for suffering.

Suffering in the Last Days

This world and the human race have been battered and bruised, crushed and torn apart, year after year down through the ages. Countless tragedies and seemingly endless atrocities fill the pages of history. But what is clear from Scripture is that there is a coming tribulation greater than all tribulations that the world has ever seen. "For nation will rise against nation, and kingdom against kingdom, and there will be famines and earthquakes in various places. All these are but the beginning of the birth pains. Then they will deliver you up to tribulation and put you to death, and you will be hated by all nations for my name's sake. And then many will fall away and betray one another and hate one another. And many false prophets will arise and lead many astray. And because lawlessness will be increased the love of many will grow cold....For then there will be great tribulation, such as has not been from the beginning of the world until now, no, and never will be" (Matt. 24:7-12, 21).

How will the church be prepared for this great suffering that is coming upon the whole earth if we cannot even handle our own personal tragedies and problems now? Dark days are coming upon this world we live in. The days are already dark, but we must be ready for the even darker days that are to come. One of my greatest fears for the Western church is that it will not be ready

---

35 C.J. Mahaney, *Living the Cross Centered Life: Keeping the Gospel the Main Thing* (Colorado Springs, CO: Multnomah Books, 2006), 99.

for the days of intensified suffering that are ahead. We must turn again to the Scriptures to check this extremely important blind spot[36] that we have missed so that we will be ready.

Types of Suffering

As we consider the great need of having a better understanding of the role of suffering in the life of a Christian and how we are to be prepared for it, it is important that we look at different types of suffering. It is obvious that we cannot take the time here to look at the vast and various forms of suffering there are in the world. Much could be mentioned in regards to suffering, from global calamities to personal losses, from natural disasters to family sicknesses, from genocide to personal abuse, from broken world systems to broken relationships. Even now as I write, I am filled with deep emotional pain due to a disappointing conversation I had a couple of days ago. But I want us to specifically take a look at three forms of suffering that I believe are significant to the Christian life in general and especially so in light of the end times.

Persecution

The first type of suffering that I want us to look at is persecution. There are different forms of persecution, but in essence the term refers to any sort of verbal, social or physical mistreatment due to one's beliefs. Jesus warned us that persecution would come to all who follow Him:

"Beware of men, for they will deliver you over to courts and flog you in their synagogues, and you will be dragged before governors and kings for my sake, to bear witness before them and the Gentiles....A disciple is not above his teacher, nor a servant above his master. It is enough for the disciple to be like his teacher,

---

36 Fernando, *The Call to Joy and Pain*, A reference to the title of chapter 8.

and the servant like his master. If they have called the master of the house Beelzebul, how much more will they malign those of his household" (Matt. 10:17-18, 24-25). "If the world hates you, know that it has hated me before it hated you. If you were of the world, the world would love you as its own; but because you are not of the world, but I chose you out of the world, therefore the world hates you. Remember the word that I said to you: 'A servant is not greater than his master.' If they persecuted me, they will also persecute you" (John 15:18-20).

Physical beatings, slander, and hatred from the world, are what we should expect as Christians. The book of Acts is filled with stories of persecution. From the arrest of Peter and John (Acts 4:3) to the arrest and beating of all the apostles (Acts 5:18, 40), from the stoning of Stephen (Acts 7:59-60) to the great persecution in Jerusalem that it stirred up (Acts 8:1), from the plot of the Jews to kill Paul in Damascus (Acts 9:23) to the killing of James and the imprisonment of Peter (Acts 12:1-5), from the opposition of Elymas the magician towards Paul and Barnabas (Acts 13:8) to the reviling from the Jews in Antioch of Pisidia (Acts 13:45), from the plots of the Jews and Gentiles against Paul and Barnabas at Iconium and the stoning of Paul at Lystra (Acts 14:5, 19) to the imprisonment and beating of Paul and Silas in Philippi (Acts 16:23), from the mob the Jews stirred up at Thessalonica and their pursuit of Paul, Silas, and Timothy at Berea (Acts 17:5, 13) to the opposition and accusation at Corinth (Acts 18:6), from the riot at Ephesus and the plots in Greece (Acts 19:28-41; 20:3) to the arrest of Paul in Jerusalem, his trials, and his banishment to Rome (Acts 21-28), it is overwhelmingly clear that persecution was a serious reality for the early church.

In 2 Corinthians 11, Paul gives us a list of the different types of persecution he received: "...imprisonments, with countless beatings, and often near death. Five times I received at the hands of the Jews the forty lashes less one. Three times I was beaten with rods. Once I was stoned....on frequent journeys...danger from my own people, danger from Gentiles, danger in the city..." (2 Cor. 11:23-26). Paul could say with confidence under the inspiration of the Holy Spirit that "all who desire to live a godly life in Christ Jesus will be persecuted" (2 Tim. 3:11). Persecution is a part of basic Christianity.

As the Church, persecution has been a part of our rich history down through the ages, from the early church to modern times. It is good for us to hear stories of the past that challenge and motivate us. One story of persecution occurred within a legion of Roman soldiers under the Roman Emperor Licinius in 320 AD. This true story goes as follows:

"The Roman governor stood resolutely before the forty Roman soldiers of the Thundering Legion. 'I command you to make an offering to the Roman gods. If you will not, you will be stripped of your military status.'

The forty soldiers all believed firmly in the Lord Jesus. They knew they must not deny Him or sacrifice to the Roman idols, no matter what the governor would do to them.

Camdidus spoke of the legion, 'Nothing is dearer or of greater honor to us than Christ our God.'

The governor then tried other tactics to get them to deny their faith. First he offered them money and imperial honors. Then he threatened them with torments and torture with the rack and with fire.

Camdidus replied, 'You offer us money that remains behind and glory that fades away. You seek to make us friends of the Emperor, but alienate us from the true King. We desire one gift, the crown of righteousness. We are anxious for one glory, the glory of the heavenly kingdom. We love honors, those of heaven.

'You threaten fearful torments and call our godliness a crime, but you will not find us fainthearted or attached to this life or easily stricken with terror. For the love of God, we are prepared to endure any kind of torture.' The governor was enraged. Now he wanted them to die a slow, painful death. They were stripped naked and herded to the middle of a frozen lake. He set soldiers to guard them to prevent any from coming to shore and escaping.

The forty encouraged each other as though they were going to battle. 'How many of our companions in arms fell on the battle front, showing themselves loyal to an earthly king? Is it possible for us to fail to sacrifice our lives in faithfulness to the true King? Let us not turn aside, O warriors, let us not turn our backs in flight from the devil.' They spent the night courageously bearing their pain and rejoicing in the hope of soon being with the Lord.

To increase the torment of the Christians, baths of hot water were put around the lake. With these the governor hoped to weaken the firm resolve of the freezing men. He told them, 'You may come ashore when you are ready to deny your faith.' In the end, one of them did weaken, came off the ice, and got into a warm bath.

When one of the guards on the shore saw him desert, he himself took the place of the traitor. Surprising everyone with the suddenness of his conversion, he threw off his clothes, and ran to join the naked ones on the ice, crying out loudly, 'I am a Christian.'"[37]

And from more recent times we read a true story of persecution in a communist area of Asia:

"The Communist soldiers had discovered their illegal Bible study.

37 *Jesus Freaks: dc Talk and the Voice of the Martyrs*, MARTYRS (Bloomington, MN: Bethany House Publishers, 1999), 96-97.

As the pastor was reading from the Bible, men with guns suddenly broke into the home, terrorizing the believers who had gathered there to worship. The Communists shouted insults and threatened to kill the Christians. The leading officer pointed his gun at the pastor's head. 'Hand me your Bible,' he demanded.

Reluctantly, the pastor handed over his Bible, his prized possession. With a sneer on his face, the guard threw the Word of God on the floor at his feet.

He glared at the small congregation. 'We will let you go,' he growled, 'but first, you must spit on this book of lies. Anyone who refuses will be shot.' The believers had no choice but to obey the officer's order.

A soldier pointed his gun at one of the men, 'you first.'

The man slowly got up and knelt down by the Bible. Reluctantly, he spit on it, praying, 'Father, please forgive me.' He stood up and walked to the door. The soldiers stood back and allowed him to leave.

'Okay, you!' the solder said, nudging the woman forward. In tears, she could barely do what the soldier demanded. She spat only a little, but it was enough. She too was allowed to leave.

Quietly, a young girl came forward. Overcome with love for her Lord, she knelt down and picked up the Bible. She wiped off the spit with her dress. 'What have they done to Your Word? Please forgive them,' she prayed.

The Communist soldier put his pistol to her head. Then he pulled the trigger."[38]

---

38 Ibid, 50-51.

These stories are both sobering and inspiring. They tell us of the great cost of following Christ and the Spirit-empowered courage it takes to stay true to our Lord. And yet this is a reality that continues in our day. It is estimated that over 160,000 people are martyred each year for the cause of Christ.[39]

Though persecution is a serious reality for much of the church, it remains unfamiliar and distant for most Christians in the West. At this writing, I am serving as a campus minister with Intervarsity Christian Fellowship at the University of Louisville in Kentucky. In the spring 2009 semester, I felt God calling me to preach the gospel out in the open every weekday for the whole semester. I learned much during this experience. But one new and unfamiliar reality I had to face was persecution. Though I have been opposed for the faith before, it was nothing like this. People shouted at me, cursed me, threatened me, and spread slanderous comments about me at various points throughout the whole semester. This is nothing compared to what many Christians face in the rest of the world, and yet I did experience true persecution. For the twelve years I have been a Christian, I have faced nothing like this.

By God's grace, through the power of the Holy Spirit, I spoke the gospel more boldly and passionately than I ever have before. And I am convinced that is the reason the persecution increased. I am convinced that a major reason the American church is not persecuted much is because our passion for the Lord has been deadened by modern comforts, and our minds are in bondage to the postmodern relativistic lies of our culture. But if we were set free from our slavery and broken off from this world's mold and were ushered into new, radical, bold, life-consuming passion for

---

39 Ron Strom, "Faith Under Fire- Group Tireless in supporting persecuted church," in WorldNet Daily, 23 June 2005; available from <http://www.wnd.com/news/article. asp?ARTICLE_ID=44911; accessed 18 May 2009.

the glory of God and the gospel of Christ, we would be hated and persecuted much, much, much more than we now are!

We will never have the chance to boldly suffer for Christ and see the fruit it will bring if we are too busy being seduced by the world. In the story of the Roman soldiers, we see the Roman governor attempt to get his soldiers to deny Christ by promising wealth and comfort if they do. Then he threatens them with loss of status and security in society and ultimately physical torture if they do not deny Him. Some of these same realities are present for Western Christians. We are not bold and radical for Christ because we are too enamored with the luxuries and comforts of this life. We are not bold and radical for Christ because we fear scarring our reputation and losing our status and security in society.

One day, not only will temptations of worldly comforts and risk of losing status in society be a present reality for American Christians, but we will also face physical threats. The reality of more intense persecution is coming to American Christians. Are we ready? There is a day coming when the church worldwide will experience intense persecution. America will not be left out. Persecution will not just be isolated to a few segments of the world. Christians from all nations will be martyred. Jesus said, "They will deliver you up to tribulation and put you to death, and you will be hated by all nations for my name's sake" (Matt. 24:9).

This coming persecution is clearly communicated in the book of Revelation. "When he opened the fifth seal, I saw under the altar the souls of those who had been slain for the word of God and for the witness they had borne. They cried out with a loud voice, 'O Sovereign Lord, holy and true, how long before you judge and avenge our blood on those who dwell on the earth?' Then they were each given a white robe and told to rest a little longer, until the number of their fellow servants and their brothers should be complete, who were to be killed as they themselves had been" (Rev. 6:9-11).

Speaking of the anti-christ, Revelation 13:7 says, "Also it was allowed to make war on the saints and to conquer them. And authority was given it over every tribe and people and language and nation…" Speaking of the coming world system known as Babylon, Revelation 17:5-6 states, "And on her forehead was written a name of mystery: 'Babylon the great, mother of prostitutes and of earth's abominations.' And I saw the woman, drunk with the blood of the saints, the blood of the martyrs of Jesus."

George Eldon Ladd, 20th century New Testament commentator, writes about the beast in Revelation 13 and its future implications: "The beast was allowed in the sovereignty of the divine purpose to exercise a worldwide authority. It is impossible to find fulfillment in these words in any historical situation in the Roman Empire of the first century. The persecution under Nero (AD 54-68) was limited to Rome and involved only a relatively few martyrs; the persecution under Domitian (AD 81-96) was of very limited scope. While occasional persecution of Christians occurred in Asia, there was nothing like a general persecution. John looks far beyond his own horizon to a time when an anti-Christian ruler will be allowed to exercise a worldwide sovereignty"[40] Tying the beast in with the woman of Revelation 17 he writes, "The woman is a fit companion for the beast who made war on the saints and conquered them (13:7). As the capital of the beast, she will be the city most noted for the persecution and martyrdom of the saints. Nothing as far-reaching as this in scope had yet befallen the Christian church….John looks for a day when the chief city of the beast will be infamous for her persecution of the saints primarily on religious grounds; nothing in

---

40 George Eldon Ladd, *A Commentary on the Revelation of John* (Grand Rapids, MI: Wm. B. Eerdmans Publishing Co., 1972), 181.

the first century provides an adequate counterpart to this. John is thinking of eschatological Babylon."[41]

This future worldwide persecution of the church is coming, and we must be prepared for it. Is the Western church ready for intensified persecution? Are we ready to face death for the sake of Christ and His gospel?

Family Division/Betrayal

Another significant aspect of suffering that often accompanies the Christian life is the tension it brings to families. It is clear from Scripture that God has designed the family and that family is a good thing (Eph. 5:22-6:4). But what is also clear is that those who begin to follow Christ within the context of an unbelieving family will experience great tension and, many times, division. Jesus said, "Do not think that I have come to bring peace to the earth. I have not come to bring peace, but a sword. For I have come to set a man against his father, and a daughter against her mother, and a daughter-in-law against her mother-in-law. And a person's enemies will be those of his own household" (Matt. 10:34-36). The world hates Christ and does not truly understand what it means to follow Him. Choosing to follow Christ in the midst of a family who does not know Him will cause tension and division.

This is a serious matter. How will we respond? Jesus warns us that "whoever loves father or mother more than me is not worthy of me, and whoever loves son or daughter more than me is not worthy of me. And whoever does not take his cross and follow me is not worthy of me" (Matt. 10:37-38). Christ will have no rivals. He is the jealous lover of our souls who died to make us His own treasured possession. He must be first in our heart, first in our mind, and first in our life. That means Christ is to be loved above family. We are to love our families, but our love for Christ

---

41 Ibid, 225.

must come first. This is where the tension comes, and this is part of the cross we will have to bear as followers of Christ.

I know of many fellow believers who have been ridiculed or ostracized by their families due to their faith in Christ. Within Muslim families, division is even more extreme when someone within the family becomes a believer. I know of one Muslim girl who came from a Muslim country to the United States to study for college. She became a believer while here. When her brothers at home found out about it, they came here and brought her back home. She was pressured to deny her faith in Christ, but she stood firm and they killed her. Her own family killed her for her faith in Christ! This should not surprise us. Jesus said, "Brother will deliver brother over to death, and the father his child, and children will rise against parents and have them put to death…" (Matt. 10:21). This is part of the cost of following Christ.

This might seem like a bizarre aspect of suffering to single out, especially in light of the Western context where family members generally are not martyred for their faith. But I want to be a step ahead of the game and warn people in advance. This is coming to all nations, including Western ones. In the end times, there will be a massive killing of Christians (Matt. 24:9) and along with this there will be a great falling away and betrayal. "Many will fall away and betray one another and hate one another" (Matt. 24:10).

Many within the church will fall away and turn against one another. People within local church communities will turn from the faith and betray fellow believers. People within culturally Christian homes will turn from Christ and rise up against each other. Christians who are a part of families that are hostile to the gospel will be murdered by their own family members. In the context of Jesus' end-times teaching, He spoke very clearly concerning this matter, saying, "And brother will deliver brother over to death, and the father his child, and children will rise against parents and have them put to death" (Mark 13:12). The days of massive worldwide betrayal and persecution among families and churches are coming.

Loss of Earthly Comforts

One other significant aspect of suffering that I want to mention is the loss of earthly comforts. Following Christ does not equal health, wealth and prosperity. Following Christ does not equal a life of comfort and ease. Does God provide for the basic needs of His children? Absolutely (Matt. 6:25-33)! But does that mean we will never have to go without? I think Scripture makes it clear that the Christian life is a life that involves the sacrifice of earthly comforts.

This call to sacrifice the comforts of this world is clearly indicated in Matthew 8:19-22: "And a scribe came up and said to him [Jesus], 'Teacher, I will follow you wherever you go.' And Jesus said to him, 'Foxes have holes, and birds of the air have nests, but the Son of Man has nowhere to lay his head.' Another of the disciples said to him, 'Lord, let me first go and bury my father.' And Jesus said to him, 'Follow me, and leave the dead to bury their own dead.'" Jesus was homeless. Following Christ sometimes involves living without a home. And following Christ sometimes involves living without the comfort of being near aging parents.

Paul makes it clear to us that he often was deprived of food and drink (2 Cor. 6:5; 11:27, Phil. 4:12). In his mission to the Gentiles, he was called to make great sacrifices, take great risks and endure much suffering for the cause of Christ (2 Cor. 11:23-28). Paul is a great example for us.

The Christian life is not peaches and cream. The Christian life involves the sacrifice of material possessions and earthly comforts. We most definitely can enjoy food, family, and the good gifts God gives in a way that glorifies Him, but this does not excuse us from the radical call to sacrifice and to do without material things for the cause of the gospel. Following Christ and being committed to His ways will not always be easy and comfortable.

An example of losing earthly comforts for the sake of Christ can be found in the person of B.B. Warfield, the Princeton professor and theologian of the late 19th and early 20th century. The following is a short account of his marriage to his wife Annie:

B. B. Warfield married his wife Annie in 1876 and they left for [their] honeymoon in Germany. He was also studying at Leipzig at that time. On a walking trip in the Harz Mountains they were overtaken by a terrible thunderstorm. It was a shattering experience for Mrs. Warfield from which she never recovered. She was more or less an invalid for the rest of her life. They had no children and Warfield cared for Annie all her days. The students would see them walking slowly together about the Seminary campus. BBW was always gentle and caring with her. He could never leave her for very long. This was one of the reasons he was rarely present at church courts or heard speaking from the floor of his presbytery. He was not outstanding in debate. His time was spent with his beloved Annie.[42]

Instead of taking the easy road of divorcing his invalid wife, B. B. Warfield chose to stay committed to their marriage covenant and take care of her for the rest of her life, thus sacrificing his own earthly comforts for the sake of honoring Christ.

If you are a Christian, you will be called upon to make sacrifices and give up earthly comforts for the sake of Christ, whether that involves the loss of home, possessions, basic necessities at times, or various other comforts that God graciously gives. We as

---

42 Geoff Thomas, "Benjamin Breckinridge Warfield- If They Do Not Do What Is Right, There May Be a Mighty Battle," in Banner of Truth Archive; available from <http://www.banneroftruth.org/pages/articles/article_detail.php?32; accessed 04 August 2009.

American Christians need to learn to get used to the idea of going without for the sake of Christ. One day we will be forced to
choose Christ or material goods in a life or death situation. The
anti-christ will demand loyalty from the whole world, and those
who do not submit to his rule will not be able to buy or sell
goods (Rev. 13:17) and will be killed (Rev. 13:15). We will have
to choose to go without and die for the sake of Christ, or we will
be disloyal to the Savior and suffer eternally. Let us be prepared
now by taking heed to the words of Martin Luther:

"Let goods and kindred go, this mortal life also, the body they
may kill, God's truth abideth still."[43]

Purpose in Suffering

At this point, it should be clear that we as Christians will face
suffering in this life just like the rest of the world, and we will also
be called to suffer in unique ways for the sake of Christ. But why?
Why does God allow such suffering? Earlier I pointed out how
God takes bad things, turns them around, and works them for good.
God has good purposes that come about in and through suffering.

This is clear in the life of Joseph who was sold into slavery by
his brothers (Gen. 37:27-28). After arriving in Egypt and becoming the overseer of his master's house, he was falsely accused of
sexual assault and put in prison (Gen. 39). Though Joseph suffered,
he was blessed by God. He interpreted the dreams of two prison-
ers (Gen. 40) and word spread to Pharaoh concerning his ability.
After interpreting Pharaoh' dream, Joseph rose to power and was
second in command to Pharaoh himself (Gen. 41). During this
time, a great famine arose in Israel and Joseph's brothers were sent
to seek provision (Gen. 41:53—42:4). Joseph reconciled with
his brothers and was reunited with his family (Gen. 45-46). He
rescued them and brought them all safely to Egypt (Gen. 46).

---

43 Martin Luther, *A Mighty Fortress is Our God.*

There was a purpose in the evil of Joseph's brothers and the suffering that came upon Joseph. It was through the suffering of Joseph that he rose to power and was able to save the people of Israel. "And God sent me before you to preserve for you a remnant on earth, and to keep alive for you many survivors" (Gen. 45:7). "As for you, you meant evil against me, but God meant it for good, to bring it about that many people should be kept alive, as they are today" (Gen. 50:20). God had good purposes in the suffering of Joseph. Ultimately, he preserved His people for the sake of the Messiah that was to come through them (Gen. 49:10).

Many other Scriptures speak of God's sovereign purposes concerning suffering. "Then Job arose and tore his robe and shaved his head and fell on the ground and worshipped. And he said, 'Naked I came from my mother's womb, and naked shall I return. The Lord gave, and the Lord has taken away; blessed be the name of the Lord.' In all this Job did not sin or charge God with wrong....Shall we receive good from God, and shall we not receive evil?" (Job 1:20-21; 2:10). "I form light and create darkness, I make well-being and create calamity, I am the Lord, who does all these things" (Isa. 45:7). "Does disaster come to a city, unless the Lord has done it?" (Amos 3:6). From Scripture, we see that God has good purposes behind suffering.

Good Purposes of Suffering

One of God's good purposes for our suffering is that it draws us closer to Him. Paul says, "For as we share abundantly in Christ's sufferings, so through Christ we share abundantly in comfort too....Indeed, we felt that we had received the sentence of death. But that was to make us rely not on ourselves but on God who raises the dead" (2 Cor. 1:5, 9). As we experience the bitter taste of suffering, we also come to experience the sweet taste of the Lord's comforting and intimate presence. It is in the deep valley of despair that we are enabled to walk more deeply into the vast recesses of His love and grace. In the place of affliction, we learn what it means to lean into His merciful heart and rely upon His strength to sustain us.

Paul's desire was that he would "share his [Christ's] sufferings" (Phil. 3:10). "Paul uses the familiar word *koinonia* in Philippians 3:10, and the literal translation is, 'the fellowship of his sufferings.' There is a depth of oneness with Christ that we can experience only through suffering."[44] To share in Christ's sufferings is to share more deeply in His satisfying love and grace. The more we are united to His suffering, the more we are united to His love.

Another good purpose behind our suffering is that it purifies us and helps make us more like Christ. Affliction was sent to Paul in order to humble him. "To keep me from becoming conceited because of the surpassing greatness of the revelations, a thorn was given me in the flesh, a messenger of Satan to harass me, to keep me from becoming conceited" (2 Cor. 12:7). The psalmist confesses that it is through affliction that he learned to obey the Word. "Before I was afflicted I went astray, but now I keep your word" (Ps. 119:67). Peter tells us that "whoever has suffered in the flesh has ceased from sin" (1 Pet. 4:1).

Suffering has a certain refining element to it. Speaking of our salvation, Peter says, "in this you rejoice, though now for a little while, if necessary, you have been grieved by various trials, so that the tested genuineness of your faith—more precious than gold that perishes though it is tested by fire—may be found to result in praise and glory and honor at the revelation of Jesus Christ" (1 Pet. 1:6-7). Trials test the genuineness of our faith in Christ and help refine and purify all those parts that do not bring praise and glory to God. Jonathan Edwards, speaking of trials and their effect on our

---

44 Fernando, *The Call to Joy and Pain*, 60.

faith, says, "…they tend to increase its beauty by establishing and confirming it, and making it more lively and vigorous, and purifying it from those things that obscured its luster and glory. As gold that is tried in the fire is purged from its alloy and all remainders of dross, and comes forth more solid and beautiful; so true faith being tried as gold is tried in the fire, becomes more precious…"[45]

Paul and James call us to rejoice in our sufferings because of the sanctifying effect they have on our lives. "We rejoice in our sufferings, knowing that suffering produces endurance, and endurance produces character, and character produces hope…" (Rom. 5:3-4). "Count it all joy, my brothers, when you meet trials of various kinds, for you know that the testing of your faith produces steadfastness. And let steadfastness have its full effect, that you may be perfect and complete, lacking in nothing" (James 1:2-4). God's good purpose is to make us more like His Son Jesus. Suffering is one of the major ingredients He uses to accomplish this end.

Another important purpose found in suffering is that it prepares us for eternity. Second Corinthians 4:16-18 says, "So we do not lose heart. Though our outer nature is wasting away, our inner nature is being renewed day by day. For this slight momentary affliction is preparing for us an eternal weight of glory beyond all comparison, as we look not to the things that are seen but to the things that are unseen. For the things that are seen are transient, but the things that are unseen are eternal." Suffering and sin will have no place in Heaven. Suffering trains us in this life to cling to Christ as our only hope and purifies us so that we will be prepared to enter a place where Christ is the center and sin is no more.

This slight momentary affliction prepares us for an eternal weight of glory by driving our eyes away from our suffering and onto the glory that is coming. When I am terribly sick, it makes

---

45 Jonathan Edwards, *The Religious Affections* (Edinburgh, UK: The Banner of Truth Trust, 2007), 22.

me long more desperately for good health. When we suffer in this life, it should create a deeper longing in us for the coming eternal pain-free enjoyment of God. We look not to the things seen (our pain) but to the things unseen (our eternal inheritance). Suffering is meant to prepare us for glory.

Not only does suffering have positive effects for the individual Christian but also for the corporate body of Christ. Suffering helps build up the church. Paul says, "Now I rejoice in my sufferings for your sake, and in my flesh I am filling up what is lacking in Christ's afflictions for the sake of his body, that is, the church" (Col. 1:24). This "does not imply that there is a deficiency in Christ's atoning death and suffering on the cross, which would contradict the central message of this letter and all the rest of Scripture as well (cf. Heb. 9:12, 24–26; 10:14)…What was 'lacking' in Christ's afflictions was the future suffering of all who (like Paul) will experience great affliction for the sake of the gospel."[46] Our suffering is a demonstration of the sacrificial love of Christ and thus helps spread the gospel and build up the church.

According to Scripture, persecution is like lighter fluid that is poured out upon the fire of Christ's messengers. Once poured out upon the church, the gospel spreads like wildfire. "And there arose on that day a great persecution against the church in Jerusalem, and they were scattered throughout the regions of Judea and Samaria… Now those who were scattered went about preaching the word" (Acts 8:1, 4). "And most of the brothers, having become confident in the Lord by my imprisonment, are much more bold to speak the word without fear" (Phil. 1:14). Persecution stirs up bold proclamation of the gospel and thus helps grow the church.

Not only does suffering help grow the church but it also helps nurture the church. Paul says, "Blessed be the God and Fa-

46 *The ESV Study Bible, English Standard Version* (ESV), (Wheaton, IL: Crossway Books, 2008), 2295.

ther of our Lord Jesus Christ, the Father of mercies and the God
of all comfort, who comforts us in all our affliction, so that we
may be able to comfort those who are in affliction, with the comfort with which we ourselves are comforted by God....If we are
afflicted, it is for your comfort and salvation..." (2 Cor. 1:3-4, 6).
Someone who is suffering will often receive more comfort talking to someone who has experienced the same thing. When we
suffer we are more authentically enabled to nurture and comfort
those within the body of Christ who are suffering.

Suffering also demonstrates the power of the gospel to a
watching world. Suffering can be a visible demonstration of the
forgiveness and radical love for enemies displayed at the cross of
Jesus. Peter explains this for us: "If when you do good and suffer
for it you endure, this is a gracious thing in the sight of God. For
to this you have been called, because Christ also suffered for you,
leaving you an example, so that you might follow in his steps. He
committed no sin, neither was deceit found in his mouth. When
he was reviled, he did not revile in return; when he suffered, he
did not threaten, but continued entrusting himself to him who
judges justly" (1 Pet. 2:20-23). As the Jews were stoning Stephen,
he "cried out with a loud voice, 'Lord, do not hold this sin against
them'" (Acts 7:60).

This radical love displayed for enemies in the midst of our
suffering is a powerful demonstration of the gospel. This is the
kind of love that we will have to pour out if we want to see many
people come to know Christ. As I mentioned earlier, I spent four
months preaching the gospel out in the open at the University of
Louisville. During this time, I encountered one guy in conversation on campus who said to me, "Just to let you know, I hate your
guts." I responded, "Well, I'm sorry you feel that way. I love you,
man." Shortly after that encounter, he came up to me while I was

preaching one day, and yelled at me with great anger. By God's grace, I responded to him with gentleness. A few weeks later, I was walking to my car and the same guy came up to me and said, "Hey Greg," in a very friendly tone. We ended up having a friendly conversation. God had softened his heart.

People want to see authenticity, especially in our postmodern culture. "People will soon get tired of today's seemingly meaningless lifestyle of living for oneself. They will ask whether they were made for something more sublime and meaningful. Then, as they see Christians considering their principles so important that they are willing to suffer for them, they may gain a new appreciation of the greatness of the gospel."[47] People need to see just how great a treasure Christ is. We will show them by how much we are willing to sacrifice and suffer for Him. Can we honestly say with the Apostle Paul, "I count everything as loss because of the surpassing worth of knowing Christ Jesus my Lord. For his sake I have suffered the loss of all things and count them as rubbish, in order that I may gain Christ" (Phil. 3:8)? Being joyful and content in the midst of loss and pain because Christ is our joy and treasure is the kind of witness that will show Christ to be supreme and worthy of following.

In this world of fickle relationships and frail love, people need to see, not only our firmly resolved commitment to Christ, but also our firmly resolved commitment to people. Paul spoke of himself as being "poured out as a drink offering upon the sacrificial offering" of the Philippians' faith (Phil. 2:17). He poured out his life and energy in committed love and service to others for the sake of Christ. This sort of love and service will call for great struggle, strain, and suffering, but the outcome will make it worth it. This is the sort of suffering that truly demonstrates the gospel and helps draw people to faith in Christ.

---

47 Fernando, *The Call to Joy and Pain*, 90.

How to Be Sustained in Suffering

Seeing the good purposes of God in our suffering will help sustain us in the midst of our suffering. As we have seen, these good purposes of suffering are revealed in the Word of God. For us to endure and be sustained in the midst of trials, we must cling to the Word of God. "If your law had not been my delight, I would have perished in my affliction" (Ps. 119:92). The prophet Jeremiah is a great example of one who suffered and clung to the Word of God in the midst of his afflictions. Jeremiah described his suffering by saying "my joy is gone; grief is upon me; my heart is sick within me…Woe is me, my mother, that you bore me" (Jer. 8:18; 15:10). But in the midst of his suffering he clung to the Word, saying to the Lord, "Your words were found, and I ate them, and your words became to me a joy and the delight of my heart" (Jer. 15:16). Let's take a look at some different meditations and realities from Scripture that will help sustain us in our journey.

The Character and Promises of God

Looking specifically to the character and promises of God will be greatly helpful in sustaining us in our suffering. If a young child were badly injured, the parents' gentle touch and reassuring words of, "It's going to be ok," would many times help sustain the child in the midst of the pain. Looking to our good heavenly Father and His reassuring promises will also help sustain us in the midst of our pain. One of the greatest promises in Scripture is found in Romans 8:28: "And we know that for those who love God all things work together for good, for those who are called according to his purpose." This promise reveals that God is sovereign, good, and wise. All suffering we face is under His control and it is controlled in such a wise and gracious way, that it will turn out for our good. Nothing in our lives is outside of His gracious and wise control. No matter what painful trial we will face, God is going to work it for our good. This truly is amazing! We must remember this truth any time we face suffering.

This promise and others lead us to behold the greatness of our trustworthy God. His promises reveal the quality of who He is. It is this sight of Him that captivates us and sustains us in the midst of pain. As David was surrounded by the darkness of war with his enemies ready to devour him, he turned his "gaze upon the beauty of the Lord" (Ps. 27:4). In the darkness of suffering, he chose to turn his eyes toward the light of God's beauty. We must look to the captivating beauty and enthralling radiance of God revealed in the face of Jesus Christ in order to be sustained and filled with joy in the midst of the ugliness of life and the darkness that surrounds us. Sustaining power in suffering must come from looking to our glorious God and His glorious promises.

The Person and Work of Jesus

Jesus is "the radiance of the glory of God and the exact imprint of his nature" (Heb. 1:3). Therefore, when we look to Jesus we see all that God the Father is. Jesus is the perfect revelation of God. When we look to the perfect revelation of God, which is Christ, we find all the grace, strength, and comfort that we need to endure suffering.

Ultimately we find grace, strength, and comfort in Christ because He entered our world to bring them to us. God the Son entered into human history as a man and faced the same temptations and sufferings that we face. He did this in order to be the faithful mediator between man and God and to relate authentically to us and help us in our time of need. "Therefore he had to be made like his brothers in every respect, so that he might become a merciful and faithful high priest in the service of God, to make propitiation for the sins of the people. For because he himself has suffered when tempted, he is able to help those who are being tempted" (Heb. 2:17-18). When we suffer we can look to Jesus, who knows what we are going through because He became one of us, suffered as we suffer (and infinitely more), and died on our behalf. He can truly relate to your pain and help you in the midst of suffering.

Because of who Jesus is and the work He has done to save us, it is impossible for us to drown in the midst of suffering. The truth is, "Christ Jesus is the one who died—more than that, who was raised—who is at the right hand of God, who indeed is interceding for us. Who shall separate us from the love of Christ? Shall tribulation, or distress, or persecution, or famine, or nakedness, or danger, or sword?" (Rom. 8:34-35). Because Jesus died for our sin, rose from the dead, ascended to the right hand of God, and is now praying for us, it is impossible for any form of suffering to tear us apart from His great love. When we suffer, and our whole world seems to be falling apart, we can take heart and know that nothing can take away from us the most precious thing in the universe, the love of Jesus. Through His work of salvation He holds us and keeps us forever. Nothing can reverse or take back the eternal redemption and mighty victory He accomplished for the people of God.

The Always-Present Ministry of the Holy Spirit

The good news is not only that Jesus sympathizes with our suffering and keeps us through our suffering, but that He actually is *with* us in the midst of our suffering. Concluding His charge given to His followers to make disciples of all nations, He says "And behold, I am with you always, to the end of the age" (Matt. 28:20). The Spirit of Christ, the Holy Spirit, lives inside all Christians and will be with us always even in the midst of the most terrible suffering. In the book of John, Jesus describes the Holy Spirit as the Helper or Comforter. The Holy Spirit helps us in all aspects of the Christian life, including providing comfort and strength in the midst of persecution and suffering. To be sustained in the midst of trials, we must remember that God's loving presence, God's powerful Spirit, lives inside us and will go through the battles with us and carry us home safely to the very end.

The Hope of Glory

Scripture reveals that one day God "will wipe away every tear from (our) eyes, and death shall be no more, neither shall there be mourning nor crying nor pain anymore" (Rev. 21:4). The more we look to that day of future glory and liberation from suffering, the more we will be sustained and strengthened in the midst of our suffering here and now. "For I consider that the sufferings of this present time are not worth comparing with the glory that is to be revealed to us....We ourselves, who have the firstfruits of the Spirit, groan inwardly as we wait eagerly for adoption as sons, the redemption of our bodies" (Rom. 8:18, 23). Anticipating the overwhelming eternal sight and experience of glory that is coming will outweigh our suffering now and cause us to look at it as no real concern. Looking to the future resurrection and our gathering to Christ will help us not lose heart in the midst of trials (2 Cor. 4:16-18).

This fixation upon future glory in the midst of suffering is modeled for us by Moses. "By faith Moses, when he was grown up, refused to be called the son of Pharaoh's daughter, choosing rather to be mistreated with the people of God than to enjoy the fleeting pleasures of sin. He considered the reproach of Christ greater wealth that the treasures of Egypt, for he was looking to the reward" (Heb. 11:24-26). This is also modeled for us by Jesus our Savior "who for the joy set before him endured the cross"

(Heb. 12:2). Looking toward being in Heaven with the Father enabled Him to endure the agony of the cross.

Jesus suffered outside the city of Jerusalem (Heb. 13:12), which was symbolic of being ostracized and shamefully cut off from the covenant people of God. May we as the radical new covenant people of God "go to him outside the camp and bear the reproach he endured. For here we have no lasting city, but we seek the city that is to come" (Heb. 13:13-14).

Prayer

Not only are we sustained in our suffering by clinging to the truths of Scripture, but also through direct communication with God by means of prayer. Very simply James says "Is anyone among you suffering? Let him pray" (James 5:13). If you were drowning, not only would it be necessary to be reminded of the principles concerning how to swim, but it would also be important to cry out for help. The same is true in our suffering. We must cling to and be reminded of the truths of Scripture, but we also must call out to God for help. Many times we are not desperate enough before God in prayer. Our pride and self-reliance get in the way. Peter tells us to "humble ourselves, therefore, under the mighty hand of God…casting all (our) anxieties on him…" (1 Pet. 5:6-7). In the midst of trials, we must learn to humble ourselves, throw ourselves before God, and express all our anxiety to Him. He is our good Father who cares for us and wants us to come to Him. Therefore, "Trust in him at all times, O people; pour out your heart before him; God is a refuge for us" (Ps. 62:8).

Throughout Scripture and especially in the Psalms we see people calling upon God in prayer in the midst of trouble. This is the way it should be. Suffering deepens our prayer life. It forces us to get real with God and teaches us how to wrestle with Him.

It teaches us how to be humble before God, how to depend on His strength, and how to trust in His goodness. Suffering teaches us how to pray with intimacy and urgency. Prayer is a dear friend that will help sustain us in our troubles.

The Church

Human beings are not designed to face suffering alone. We are relational creatures who need each other. We need the church in order to be sustained in our suffering. We are not to face suffering in isolation, but together with the body of Christ. "For just as the body is one and has many members, and all the members of the body, though many, are one body, so it is with Christ. For in one Spirit we were all baptized into one body…If one member suffers, all suffer together" (1 Cor. 12:12-13, 26). We are commanded to "weep with those who weep" (Rom. 12:15). We are to face our trials together as one body of Christ.

Our local church community should be the place where we can be upheld in our time of need. We are commanded to look out for our fellow believers' needs and to be there for them in their pain. "Contribute to the needs of the saints and seek to show hospitality" (Rom. 12:13). Our local church should be the place where we give and receive words of comfort and prayers of encouragement in the midst of affliction. It should be the place where physical needs are met in the midst of trying times. The sending of Timothy to the church in Thessalonica in order to provide exhortation and comfort in the midst of persecution (1 Thess. 3:2-3) and the call for the elders of the church to pray for the sick (James 5:14) show us the great importance and need we have for the church in the midst of suffering. May we as the body of Christ continually learn how to help comfort and strengthen one another in times of need.

How to Respond to Suffering

So far we have looked at some of the different types of suffering and how they relate to the end times. We have looked at the good purposes of God found in suffering and the means that are necessary in order to be sustained in our suffering. Finally, we want to look at how we are to respond to suffering. We have already seen that we must cling to the Word, cry out to the Lord in prayer, and seek comfort and strength through the church, but Scripture gives us many other specific ways we are to respond to suffering.

1. Trust in the Lord and do not be anxious. "You keep him in perfect peace whose mind is stayed on you, because he trusts in you. Trust in the Lord forever, for the Lord God is an everlasting rock" (Isa. 26:3-4). In the midst of trials of all kinds and degrees, we must cling to and trust our sovereign and good God. He will be our strong and immovable rock who gives us stability and peace in the storms of life. This peace and stability in the midst of suffering is available to all those who are in Christ. That is why we are told: "do not be anxious about anything, but in everything by prayer and supplication with thanksgiving let your requests be made known to God. And the peace of God, which surpasses all understanding, will guard your hearts and your minds in Christ Jesus" (Phil. 4:6-7). Jesus knowing our anxious tendencies also said, "…do not be anxious about your life, what you will eat, nor about your body, what you will put on….Seek his kingdom, and these things will be added to you" (Lk. 12:22, 31). When times are tough and finances are low, we know God will provide for all our basic needs. Therefore, we must not worry. In the midst of the current global economic problems, we do not have to worry. He is our good Father and will provide for all that we truly need.

2. Do not fear. When we face persecutors, Jesus tells us to "have no fear of them…do not fear those who kill the body but cannot kill the soul" (Matt. 10:26, 28). "Do not fear what you are about to suffer. Behold, the devil is about to throw some of you into prison, that you may be tested, and for ten days you will have tribulation. Be faithful unto death, and I will give you the crown of life" (Rev. 2:10). "Fear not, for I have redeemed you; I have called you by name, you are mine. When you pass through the waters, I will be with you; and through the rivers, they shall not overwhelm you; when you walk through the fire you shall not be burned, and the flame shall not consume you" (Isa. 43:2-3). Whatever opposition or trials we face, God will be with us, and He will carry us through to the end and bring us home to glory. Therefore, we must not fear.

3. Boldly proclaim the gospel. In the face of persecution we are not to cower down, but we are to boldly speak the truth. Jesus said, "What I tell you in the dark, say in the light, and what you hear whispered, proclaim on the housetops" (Matt. 10:27). Peter is a great example for us to follow in boldly speaking for Christ in the face of opposition. After healing a lame man, preaching the gospel, and then being arrested for it, Peter and John were questioned by the authorities concerning their faith in Christ. Listen to the boldness in Peter's response: "Peter, filled with the Holy Spirit, said to them, 'Rulers of the people and elders, if we are being examined today concerning a good deed done to a crippled man, by what means this man has been healed, let it be known to all of you and to all the people of Israel that by the name of Jesus Christ of Nazareth, whom you crucified, whom God raised from the dead—by him this man is standing before you well. This Jesus is the stone that was rejected by you, the builders, which has become the cornerstone. And there is salvation in no one else, for there is no other name under heaven given among men by which we must be saved'" (Acts 4:8-12). After this incident, they were threatened some more and released from prison. In boldness the believers prayed, went on speaking the word, and were arrested again for it. They were brought before the authorities and were reminded that they were previously commanded to not preach Jesus. Peter responded again with boldness saying, "We must obey God rather than men" (Acts 5:29).

When faced with opposition, may we respond like Peter and unashamedly proclaim the good news of Jesus. May we be like Jeremiah who said, "If I say, 'I will not mention him, or speak any more in his name,' there is in my heart as it were a burning fire shut up in my bones, and I am weary of holding it in, and I cannot" (Jer. 20:9). By the power of the Holy Spirit, may our hearts be filled with a fiery passion for the gospel that explodes through our mouths with bold proclamation, even in the face of death.

4. Love your enemies. Jesus said, "I say to you who hear, Love your enemies, do good to those who hate you, bless those who curse you, pray for those who abuse you" (Lk. 6:27-28). As followers of Jesus Christ we are different from the world. We are not to respond to opposition with revenge and retaliation. We are to be loving and kind to those who mistreat us. We are to do good to them, bless them, and pray for them, wishing no ill upon them.

5. Rejoice and do not grumble. Jesus said, "Blessed are you when others revile you and persecute you and utter all kinds of evil against you falsely on my account. Rejoice and be glad, for your reward is great in heaven" (Matt. 5:11-12). First Peter 4:13-14 states, "Rejoice insofar as you share Christ's sufferings, that you may also rejoice and be glad when his glory is revealed. If you are insulted for the name of Christ, you are blessed, because the Spirit of glory and of God rests upon you." We are to rejoice in being "counted worthy to suffer dishonor for the name" (Acts 5:41). It truly is an honor to suffer for Jesus. Therefore, we must rejoice!

Not only are we to rejoice in the face of persecution, but we are to be joyful in the midst of all forms of suffering. "Count it all joy, my brothers, when you meet trials of various kinds" (James 1:2). Having joy in the midst of trials shows people that Christ is our treasure and the foundation that holds us together. Being content and joyful in suffering is a powerful witness to the world. Paul tells us, "Do all things without grumbling or questioning, that you may be blameless and innocent, children of God without blemish in the midst of a crooked and twisted generation, among whom you shine as lights in the world" (Phil. 2:14-15). We as Western Christians need to wake up and realize just how much we complain and how it ruins our witness to the world. By God's grace, we must learn to be content and free from complaining in the midst of inconvenience and every form of suffering.

6. Faith and Endurance. In light of the intense persecution from the anti-christ that is coming, we are charged with these words: "Here is a call for the endurance and faith of the saints" (Rev. 13:10). In the midst of suffering and intense persecution, we must cling to Christ with unflinching faith and press on, persevering in His strength. After mentioning the great faith and suffering of the Old Testament saints, we are told: "Therefore, since we are surrounded by so great a cloud of witnesses, let us also lay aside every weight, and sin which clings so closely, and let us run with endurance the race that is set before us, looking to Jesus, the founder and perfecter of our faith, who for the joy set before him endured the cross, despising the shame, and is seated at the right hand of the throne of God. Consider him who endured from sinners such hostility against himself, so that you may not grow weary or fainthearted" (Heb. 12:1-3). May we look to the saints of old and our Savior, Jesus, who remained firm in faith and persevered in the face of intense affliction. May we never give up, and may we never take our eyes off Christ in this sometimes grueling race we are running, for we know that only "the one who endures to the end will be saved" (Matt. 24:13).

An Exhortation: Be Ready to Suffer and Help Make Others Ready

Are you prepared for suffering? If small or great personal trials were to come upon you soon, would you be ready for them? And if you are not ready to face your own personal trials, how will you face the great global trials that are to come if you are still alive? Great global calamities are coming that the world has never seen (Matt. 24:3-31; Rev. 6; 8-9; 16). These epic worldwide disasters will shake and horrify the whole world. Would you be ready for them if they were to come soon? Are you helping other people to be ready? By God's grace, may we all be ready and help other people get ready.

A Word to Pastors

Those of you who are pastors are called to "shepherd the flock of God that is among you" (1 Pet. 5:2). Part of shepherding the flock means that you are to protect your people. But protect them from what? You will not be called always to protect them from physical suffering, but you will be called to protect them from spiritual suffering, by preparing them to endure the various trials that may come their way. I plead with you to preach and teach and counsel and lead in such a way that by God's grace they will cling to Christ and endure in the midst of whatever afflictions come their way. Great afflictions are coming and you must prepare them.

> "Times are coming when shepherds will say again to their flock, as they have done in days gone by, 'Do not fear what you are about to suffer. Behold, the devil is about to throw some of you into prison, that you may

be tested, and for ten days you will have tribulation. Be faithful unto death, and I will give you the crown of life' (Rev. 2:10). I am deeply thankful for Christian counseling to make my marriage better. But in addition, I need a shepherd who will tell me: 'The devil may kill you, but that's okay. Jesus will give you the crown of life.' Along with the tender words of daily blessings, I need the tough warning that the Beast will win. For a season. '(The Beast) was allowed to make war on the saints and to conquer them...and...cause those who would not worship the image of the beast to be slain' (Rev. 13:7, 15). I need the warning that the great Babylonian whore will one day be 'drunk with the blood of the saints, the blood of the martyrs of Jesus' (Rev. 17:6).

These horrors are in the Bible. God's Word. Where is the shepherd who is preparing the saints for this kind of future? What answer could he give to our questions? What answer would fit with the upbeat entertainment mood? ...The fact that people do not feel a need for this kind of food in their spiritual diet should not silence the wise and loving shepherd. Our felt needs are about to change dramatically. Pastors will be glad if they are ahead of the curve. Otherwise, it may be too late. Coddled people will not be good listeners when their world collapses. They will be numb with confusion and rage at the God who wasn't supposed to allow this."[48]

May all pastors and church leaders take heed to these sobering words and begin to prepare their flocks for what is to come.

---

48 John Piper, *Spectacular Sins and Their Global Purpose in the Glory of Christ* (Wheaton, IL: Crossway Books, 2008), 15-16. Used by permission of Crossway, a publishing ministry of Good News Publishers, Wheaton, IL 60187, www.crossway.org.

A Psalm of Comfort—Psalm 46

"God is our refuge and strength, a very present help in trouble. Therefore we will not fear though the earth gives way, though the mountains be moved into the heart of the sea, though its waters roar and foam, though the mountains tremble at its swelling. *Selah*

There is a river whose streams make glad the city of God, the holy habitation of the Most High. God is in the midst of her; she shall not be moved; God will help her when morning dawns. The nations rage, the kingdoms totter; he utters his voice, the earth melts. The LORD of hosts is with us; the God of Jacob is our fortress. *Selah*

Come, behold the works of the LORD, how he has brought desolations on the earth. He makes wars cease to the end of the earth; he breaks the bow and shatters the spear; he burns the chariots with fire. "Be still, and know that I am God. I will be exalted among the nations, I will be exalted in the earth!" The LORD of hosts is with us; the God of Jacob is our fortress. *Selah*"

CHAPTER 6

Proclaim the Gospel to Every Nation— Finish the Task!

In this book, we have focused on our urgent need to be prepared for the Lord's return. We have talked about our great need to grow in longing for His Second Coming. We have discussed the importance of loving the truth and growing in holiness. We have talked about how to use our time well and how to be prepared for suffering. These are extremely important, but what about the unreached nations?

How are we reaching out to prepare other people for the return of Jesus? How are we reaching out to prepare the unreached peoples of the world for the Second Coming of Christ? The Western Church has done much towards the cause of world missions. Let us not forget that. And yet much of the Western Church today is plagued with consumer-driven Christianity. We treat the church like a product simply to be consumed for our own personal enjoyment. We take, take and take. It's all about me and God and how I can be spiritually nourished and fulfilled. Naturally we are all inclined to be self-oriented and to look inwardly rather than outwardly. But this is not the whole picture of biblical Christianity. Biblical Christianity is about radical mission.

The true Christian faith is radically oriented toward the nations. It's about forsaking comfort and going to places that have never heard the good news of Jesus, so that God's glory may spread across the whole earth.

God's Heart and Plan for the Nations

When many think of missions, they think of the great commission given by Jesus in Matthew 28 or the missionary journeys of Paul to the Gentiles in the book of Acts. Many Christians look primarily to the New Testament when thinking about missions, and rightfully so. But what we need to realize is that God has always had a heart and plan for the nations. He has always had a plan to save a people for Himself from all peoples of the world. When we realize this, we realize how central and important the cause of world missions really is.

We see God's heart and plan for the nations revealed early in the course of history. In Genesis 12:1-3 "Now the Lord said to Abram, 'Go from your country and your kindred and your father's house to the land that I will show you. And I will make of you a great nation, and I will bless you and make your name great, so that you will be a blessing. I will bless those who bless you, and him who dishonors you I will curse, and in you all the families of the earth shall be blessed.'" Here God chooses to pour out this amazing blessing upon Abraham that will ultimately spread to the nations.

What is this great blessing that Abraham received from God and that will eventually go to all the nations? Part of the blessing he received would be that he would have many physical descendants, greater than the dust of the earth and the stars of the heavens (Gen. 13:16; 15:5). He would be made into a great nation, the nation of Israel. He and his descendants would also receive a land to call home (Gen. 13:14-15). But the greatest of all blessings would be his covenant relationship with God.

A covenant is a binding agreement. God's covenant with Abraham included the giving of descendants and land, but the ultimate and central blessing of the covenant was a permanent binding love relationship with God. "I will establish my covenant between me and you and your offspring after you throughout their generations for an everlasting covenant, to be God to you and to your offspring after you" (Gen. 17:7). Though God initiated this covenant, Abraham entered it by faith (Gen. 15:6).

Yet the amazing thing is that this covenant relationship with God was not just for Abraham and the Jews but would eventually come to all nations: "…In you all the families of the earth shall be blessed" (Gen. 12:3). Christ, the offspring of Abraham, would be the fulfillment of this covenant, thus ushering the nations into this new relationship with God through faith in Him (Gal. 4:5-7). God had a heart and plan for the nations from the beginning. He brought this plan to fulfillment in Christ.

In the Old Testament, God chose to supremely set His love and affection upon the people of Israel, but even in the Old Testament we get glimpses of His heart for the world, thus pointing us to the ingathering of the nations into the covenant that would come after the Messiah. God tells the Israelites how to treat the foreigner who travels with them. "When a stranger sojourns with you in your land, you shall not do him wrong. You shall treat the stranger who sojourns with you as the native among you, and you shall love him as yourself, for you were strangers in the land of Egypt: I am the Lord your God" (Lev. 19:33-34).

In the story of Ruth, we see a Moabite woman redeemed out of poverty and distress and brought into marriage with an Israelite. She commits herself to the Lord and the Lord's people and she is accepted as a part of the people of God. Ruth, speaking to Naomi her mother-in-law, said, "Your people shall be my people, and your God my God" (Ruth 1:16). The elders of Israel, speaking about Ruth, said, "May the Lord make the woman, who is coming into your house, like Rachel and Leah, who together built up the house of Israel" (Ruth 4:11). Christ Himself would eventually be a descendant of Ruth (Matt. 1:5).

In the Psalms, a desire and calling for the nations to worship the Lord is evident. "Let the peoples praise you, O God; let all the peoples praise you! Let the nations be glad and sing for joy… Declare his glory among the nations, his marvelous works among all the peoples! Ascribe to the Lord, O families of the peoples, ascribe to the Lord glory and strength" (Ps. 67:3-4; 96:3, 7). King Solomon, in his prayer of dedication for the temple, prayed, "Likewise, when a foreigner, who is not of your people Israel, comes from a far country for your name's sake… when he comes and prays toward this house, hear in heaven your dwelling place and do according to all for which the foreigner calls to you, in order that all the peoples of the earth may know your name and fear you, as do your people Israel" (1 Kings 8:41-43).

God sent Jonah the prophet to Nineveh to warn the inhabitants of judgment. After Jonah complained about God's mercy on the people of Nineveh, God responded by saying, "Should not I pity Nineveh, that great city, in which there are more than 120,000 persons who do not know their right hand from their left" (Jonah 4:11).

Isaiah the prophet points preeminently to the coming Messiah who would be "a light for the nations" so that God's "salvation may reach to the end of the earth" (Isa. 42:6; 49:6). Isaiah also shows us what will be the final outcome of God's plan for the nations. "It shall come to pass in the latter days that the mountain of the house of the Lord shall be established as the highest of the mountains, and shall be above the hills; and all the nations shall flow to it, and many peoples shall come, and say: 'Come, let us go up to the mountain of the Lord, to the house of the God of Jacob, that he may teach us his ways and that we may walk in his paths.' For out of Zion shall go the law, and the word of the Lord from Jerusalem. He shall judge between the nations, and shall decide disputes for many peoples; and they shall beat their swords into plowshares, and their spears into pruning hooks; nation shall not lift up sword against nation, neither shall they learn war anymore" (Isa. 2:2-4).

King Jesus has come, bringing salvation through His death and resurrection for all the nations, and one day He will come again bringing the fullness of His kingdom of righteousness and peace. In that day, all nations will flow to this most high and exalted kingdom.

Though the Old Testament clearly points to God's heart and plan for the nations, the true reality of it was hidden until the time of the apostles. Paul writes, "…the mystery was made known to me by revelation…This mystery is that the Gentiles are fellow heirs, members of the same body, and partakers of the promise in Christ Jesus through the gospel" (Eph. 3:3, 6). Paul elaborates further and says, "To me…this grace was given, to preach to the Gentiles the unsearchable riches of Christ, and to bring to light for everyone what is the plan of the mystery hidden for ages in God who created all things, so that through the church the manifold wisdom of God might now be made known to the rulers and authorities in the heavenly places. This was according to the eternal purpose that he has realized in Christ Jesus our Lord" (Eph. 3:8-11). Here we see that God had a mysterious hidden plan to save sinners from all nations, which He fulfilled in Christ and revealed to Paul. This mysterious plan of saving the nations was "hidden for ages" and was a part of God's "eternal purpose" (Eph. 3:9, 11). What this shows us is that God's plan to save sinners from all nations does not even begin in the Old Testament but is found in the eternal mind of God before He created the world (Eph. 1:3-4). Since missions is a part of the eternal mind and heart of God, it must be of central importance to us.

This mission to go to all nations is so important that it was a part of Jesus' last words on earth. "All authority in heaven and on earth has been given to me. Go therefore and make disciples of all nations" (Matt. 28:18-19). "You will be my witnesses in Jerusalem and in all Judea and Samaria, and to the end of the earth" (Acts 1:8).

The final picture we see in the Bible is one of all nations standing before God and Christ in worship. "I looked, and behold, a great multitude that no one could number, from every nation, from all tribes and peoples and languages, standing before the throne and before the Lamb, clothed in white robes, with palm branches in their hands, and crying out with a loud voice, 'Salvation belongs to our God who sits on the throne, and to the Lamb'" (Rev. 7:9-10)! From the beginning to the end, God is about the nations. From start to finish, God is shown to be a missionary God who calls His people to join His mission.

Defining the Task: What Is Our Mission?

From the Scriptures, it is clear as crystal that God is a missionary God and that He calls His people to join Him on a mission. But what exactly is the mission that God has called us to? Obviously there are many things that we are called to do in the Christian life. But what is the specific mission or commission that God and His Son, Jesus Christ, have given to us, the church? The mission we have been given is to proclaim the gospel of Jesus Christ, make disciples of Him and establish churches among all nations for the glory of God.

Yet the sad and terrifying truth is that a large majority of the church in the West seems to be unclear concerning this mission that we have been given. Many Christians see missions as simply building houses in Mexico or volunteering at an orphanage in Ghana. I can't count how many times I've heard of churches taking short-term "mission trips," where all they end up doing is the same humanitarian work that an atheist could do. I'm not saying we shouldn't do works of social justice. It is clear from Scripture that we *must* pursue these sorts of good deeds. What I am saying, is that social justice is not the great commission that Jesus gave us. Let me be as plain as possible. Unless the heart of your short-term "mission trip" (or long-term work) involves proclaiming the gospel or making disciples and establishing churches, you have not done mission work according to the Scriptures. You may have done some good deeds, but you have not brought people the hope of Christ.

Jesus' words to the disciples He encountered on the road to Emmaus after His resurrection, clarify the mission we have been given. "…He opened their minds to understand the Scriptures, and said to them, 'Thus it is written, that the Christ should suffer and on the third day rise from the dead, and that repentance and forgiveness of sins should be *proclaimed* in his name to all nations, beginning from Jerusalem. You are my witnesses of these things" (Luke 24:45-48, emphasis mine). Our mission is to be a witness of Jesus Christ. To be a witness of Jesus Christ, means we have to *proclaim* who He is (…"the Christ"), what He has done to save sinners (…"Christ should suffer and on the third day rise from the dead"), and how all the nations must respond to Him and thus be forgiven and reconciled to God (…"repentance and forgiveness of sins should be proclaimed in his name to all nations").

Luke takes us again to this commission Jesus gives to the church in Acts 1:8 where the final words of Christ are recorded before He ascends to heaven. "…You will receive power when the Holy Spirit has come upon you, and you will be my *witnesses* in Jerusalem and in all Judea and Samaria, and to the end of the earth" (Acts 1:8, emphasis mine). Here again we see this word 'witnesses.' To be a witness is to testify about something you have seen or know to be true. Luke 24:45-48 and Acts 1:8 are connected in emphasizing the commission that Jesus has given the church, which is to be a *witness* of Him and what He has done. To be a witness of Christ according to Luke 24:45-48, Acts 1:8, and the entire book of Acts, is to testify and *proclaim* what we know to be true, that Jesus is the Savior and Lord of the universe who died on the cross for our sin and rose again so that people from all nations who repent and trust in Him would be forgiven and reconciled to God.

This central mission of proclaiming the good news of Christ can be found throughout the entire book of Acts. In fact, in almost every chapter of Acts you see some form of proclamation. The Greek word for preaching, "*euaggelizo*," occurs fifteen times in the book. The Greek word for proclaiming, "*kerysso*," occurs eight times. The Greek word for speaking forth, "*apophtheggomai*," occurs three times.

Is it true that being a witness for Christ involves more than proclamation? Absolutely. Throughout the book of Acts you see that miracles are closely tied to the preaching of the gospel. These miracles testify to the power of the gospel. In Acts, as well as throughout the Scriptures, you see the importance of Christians having lives of holiness, love, and service to one another and the lost. This must go along with what it means to be a witness sent out on mission for Christ. But what the church needs to realize is that good deeds done for people will not save anyone. We must open our mouths and proclaim Christ and Him crucified for sinners! Billions of people around the world are lost and on their way to eternal torment in hell! May we have the same "great sorrow and unceasing anguish" in our hearts for the lost as Paul did (Rom. 9:2). A countless number of eternal destinies are at stake. Unless the nations call upon Christ, they will not be saved. "But how are they to call on him in whom they have not believed? And how are they to believe in him of whom they have never heard? And how are they to hear without someone preaching? And how are they to preach unless they are sent? As it is written, 'How beautiful are the feet of those who preach the good news!'" (Rom. 10:14-15).

The mission Christ has given to the church is to proclaim the gospel to all nations. The church of Acts was not perfect. But if you read carefully through that book, you will see a heavy evangelistic zeal and emphasis on proclaiming the gospel of Jesus that the church in the West desperately needs to imitate.

Yet proclaiming the good news of Jesus is not all that there is concerning the heart of the mission Christ has given to the church. In Matthew 28:18-20, Jesus put His commission to the church this way: "All authority in heaven and on earth has been given to me. Go therefore and *make disciples* of all nations, baptizing them in the name of the Father and of the Son and of the Holy Spirit, *teaching* them to observe all that I have commanded you. And behold, I am with you always, to the end of the age" (emphasis mine). Not only are we to tell people how they can get right with God through Jesus, but we need to also train and teach those who have become Christians how to grow in loving God and reflecting Christ in their lives. We have been commissioned not just to make converts but to make disciples. We have been commanded not just to help people become Christians but to help people become mature Christians. Throughout Acts we see the importance of making mature disciples of Christ (Acts 11:26; 14:21-22; 15:35-36, 41; 18:11, 23; 19:9-10).

This call for us to go to all nations and make disciples must not be divorced from the local church. Like a fish out of water, we will spiritually die without Christian community. We were made for community and without community we will not grow as Christians. God has instituted the local church to be the means by which discipleship takes place. In Acts, being discipled or trained up in the faith, occurs in the context of other believers. Wherever there were believers, they gathered together in congregations. Churches were planted and established and leaders were appointed as the God-given means for people to grow in their knowledge and love for God (Acts 14:21-23).

Proclaiming the gospel of Jesus, making disciples, and establishing churches among all nations for the glory of God is the great commission and mission Christ has given to the church. This mission must be obeyed and is vital for the health of the church.

The Primacy of Unreached People Groups

Mission indeed is at the heart of Christianity. In some sense of the word, all Christians are missionaries. All Christians are called to be "ambassadors for Christ" (2 Cor. 5:20), wherever they go. Every Christian has joined the mission of God and has the responsibility to boldly proclaim the gospel and love the lost in whatever context God has placed them or called them. Whether that means one's hometown, the place one works, the place one goes to school, the inner city, or another country, all Christians are called to be on mission carrying the message of God's grace found in Jesus Christ.

Wherever there is a need for Christ, Christians should be seeking to meet that need. And there is a need for Christ everywhere. Though this is true, there are places that have a greater need than others. Though all places of the world have a need for Christ, there is a sense in which the places of greatest need should have the greatest priority. For example, let's say a house with people in it is on fire just north of the gulf coast of Florida. Firefighters are on the scene, and more are being sent to help put out the fire and rescue the victims. While this is going on, a massive hurricane comes crashing into the coast just miles away leaving thousands in desperate need of rescue. Instead of sending more firefighters to that one house north of the coast, they are redirected to help rescue the thousands affected by the hurricane. This is the way it should be with missions.

There is a need for mission work everywhere, but some places have greater need and therefore greater priority than other places. Though this is true, this does not reflect the current reality in world missions. In fact, less than 10% of missionaries actually go to people groups where there is no gospel witness or there are no churches established.[49]

What do we mean by the term "people group?" "A People Group is 'a significantly large grouping of individuals who perceive themselves to have a common affinity for one another because of their shared language, religion, ethnicity, residence, occupation, class or caste, situation, etc., or combinations of these.'"[50] This broadens the needs of the world and also intensifies the missionary task. This definition of "people group" also more clearly captures the meaning of Jesus command for us to "Go, make disciples of all 'nations'…" (emphasis mine). The word for, 'nations,' in Greek, is *ethne*, which refers more specifically to ethno-linguistic groups of people. The missionary task is not just confined to going to all geo-political nations, but all the specific ethnic groups of the world.

---

49 Ralph D. Winter and Bruce A. Koch, "Finishing the Task: The Unreached Peoples Challenge," in *Perspectives On The World Christian Movement*, ed. Ralph D. Winter and Steven C. Hawthorne. 4th ed. (Pasadena, CA: William Carey Library, 2009), 543.
50 Ibid, 536.

There are 16, 308 people groups in the world today and 6,631 of those people groups are unreached.[51] "An Unreached People Group is 'a people group within which there is no indigenous community of believing Christians able to evangelize this people group.'"[52] And the tragedy is that less than 10% of missionaries are going to these unreached people groups. Most missionaries go to places and work with people groups where there are already lots of Christians and churches. This has to change. Going to these already reached places to disciple and train is important, but I believe as a whole the unreached people groups should have our greatest priority and sense of urgency.

This was the case for the Apostle Paul who said, "from Jerusalem and all the way around to Illyricum I have fulfilled the ministry of the gospel of Christ; and thus I make it my ambition to preach the gospel, not where Christ has already been named, lest I build on someone else's foundation" (Rom. 15:19-20). Once Paul established the work in the places he went, he decided to move on and preach the gospel where Christ had not yet been mentioned. He made this his ambition, the driving force of his life and mission. What about us? Do you have a burning desire and passion to see people groups who have never even heard the name of Jesus be brought out of darkness into the light of Christ's glorious grace?

Seeing things with God's perspective and with God's heart will help us realize the great priority of going to the unreached/unengaged people groups of the world. At the cross of Jesus, we see God's passion for every lost people group of the world. Speaking of Jesus, Revelation 5:9 says, "by your blood you ransomed people for God from every tribe and language and people and nation." At the cross, Jesus bought a people for God's own trea-

---

51 Joshua Project, 29 July 2009, available from <www.joshuaproject.org; accessed 04 August 2009.
52 Winter and Koch, "Finishing the Task: The Unreached Peoples Challenge," in *Perspectives On The World Christian Movement*, 536.

sured possession from every people group in the world. He died to free people bound in darkness from every tribe, language, people, and nation. God's passion and plan for the unreached peoples of the world is firmly displayed at the cross. It is as though Jesus shouts out to us with a battle cry from the cross saying, "Go get my people!" And it is certain, what Christ accomplished on the cross 2,000 years ago will be brought to fulfillment before He returns. We must go with great urgency to the unreached so that we can see our King.

Missions and the Second Coming

Many Christians look at the Second Coming of Jesus as something we just sit around and wait for. This could not be further from the truth. The reason Christ has not come back yet is because in our laziness and complacency we have not finished the task He has called us to. Jesus said, "This gospel of the kingdom will be proclaimed throughout the whole world as a testimony to all nations, and then the end will come" (Matt. 24:14). The good news and free offer to sinners to come live under the reign of Christ's grace and power is to be spread and established among all nations (*ethne*) or all ethnic groups. Once this takes place then the end will come. Once all the people Christ died to save from every tribe, language, people, and nation come into the kingdom by faith (Rev. 5:9-10), King Jesus will return to the earth. This anticipation for the Lord's return should propel us forward to take action.

"Do you love the Lord's appearing? Then you will bend every effort to take the gospel into all the world. It troubles me in the light of the clear teaching of God's Word, in the light of our Lord's explicit definition of our task in The Great Commission, that we take it so lightly….His is the kingdom; He reigns in heaven, and He manifests His reign on earth in and through His church. When we have accomplished our mission, He will return and establish His kingdom in glory. To us it is given not only to wait for but also to hasten the coming of the day of God."[53]

Christ will not return until all the unreached people groups are reached. By God's grace, let us go and reach them so that He may come!

How to Get Involved in this Great Mission

As we see the utmost importance and urgency of world missions, the question should then become, "how do I get involved in missions?" "Not everyone is called to be a missionary. But missions is for everyone."[54] Not all Christians are called to go overseas, but all Christians are called to play a part in fulfilling the Great Commission in some way. So what are some practical ways we can get involved with missions and play our part?

The first step we can take in getting involved with missions is to learn about missions. Taking a class like "Perspectives on the World Christian Movement," which is offered at churches in various cities throughout the U.S., could be a great place to start. Reading missionary biographies or studying the history of missions could also be helpful. Building relationships with internationals in your city, learning their culture, and sharing the love of Christ with them is an extremely valuable way to get involved with missions. Researching people groups online through websites like Joshua Project or spending time with missionaries on furlough could also be great ways to get involved.

A second way to be involved with world missions is to pray for the nations. Get a map of the world or a list of all the unreached people groups and spend time daily praying for the different regions and peoples of the world. Pray for missionaries in your

---

53 George Eldon Ladd, *The Gospel of the Kingdom: Scriptural Studies in the Kingdom of God* (Grand Rapids: Wm. B. Eerdmans Publishing, Co., 1959), 139-140.
54 Steve Saint, "Introduction," in *The Missionary Call*, by David Sills (Chicago: Moody Publishers, 2008), 11.

church. Start a prayer group at church that focuses on praying for the unreached. Prayer will be the key to finishing the missionary task. Do not underestimate the power and importance of prayer.

A third and crucial way to be involved with missions is to give financially to missionaries or missionary agencies that are at work spreading the gospel among the nations. It has been estimated that less than 1% of funds from Western churches actually goes to mission work with unreached people groups. This is sad. Generous and sacrificial giving towards the cause of missions will be necessary for the task to move forward. In some sense, senders are just as important as those who go.

A fourth and obvious way to be involved with missions is to go to the nations. Jesus calls us to "*Go* and make disciples of all nations" (emphasis mine). Some Christians are called to be foreign missionaries. Some will be called to leave their home culture and enter into a new and unfamiliar culture for the sake of the gospel. And yet how does someone know if he or she is called to go be a missionary overseas? "What is the missionary call? How are we to understand it? The missionary call includes an awareness of the needs of a lost world, the commands of Christ, a concern for the lost, a radical commitment to God, your church's affirmation, blessing and commissioning, a passionate desire, the Spirit's gifting, and an indescribable yearning that motivates beyond all understanding."[55]

What about you? Is God calling you to go overseas to do missions? The church is still in desperate need for more radical and bold witnesses to rise up and go to the unreached peoples of the world. Could God be drawing you in this direction? Go on a short term trip, read about missions, and expose yourself before the Lord in prayer as you begin to discern God's direction for your life.

---

55 David Sills, *The Missionary Call*, 30.

A fifth way to get involved with missions is to mobilize others. Raising awareness of the needs in the world and providing resources for those interested in missions is an important aspect of contributing to the cause of world missions. Pointing people to missions materials, teaching others about missions, and providing training for skills needed on the field are all key ways to be active in the Great Commission. Leading a short-term trip can also be a great way to mobilize and equip others for missions.

What is important is that we remember that "God has called every Christian to international missions, but He does not want everyone to go. God calls some to be senders. If everyone were to pack up and go, who would send, pray, and continue the ministries we leave behind? Conversely, if we all stayed to send [others], there would be no one to go. God calls others to be goers."[56] What is God's role for you in world missions?

The Cost and Reward of Missions

As we consider God's heart for the nations, the importance and urgency of the task, as well as the practical ways we can get involved, we must also stop to consider the great cost and reward of missions. This cost and reward is clearly identified in Mark 10:28-30: "Peter began to say to him (Jesus), 'See, we have left everything and followed you.' Jesus said, 'Truly, I say to you, there is no one who has left house or brothers or sisters or mother or father or children or lands, for my sake and for the gospel, who will not receive a hundredfold now in this time, houses and brothers and sisters and mothers and children and lands, with persecutions, and in the age to come eternal life.'" There is no sugar coating it. The life of mission for Christ comes at a cost and requires great sacrifice. The life of the disciples and the life of the foreign missionary involve leaving behind everything that one holds dear. It

---

56 Ibid, 58-59.

involves leaving behind the comfort of family and home for the sake of Jesus and His glorious gospel. With these sacrifices in the cause of missions also comes persecution and hardship.

But with the cost of missions also comes great reward. Through the loss of family and home, in the midst of persecution and hardship, a new family and a new home is gained. Though we lose the material and familial comforts of home in the cause of missions, God still provides for our physical, emotional, and spiritual needs. He will supply us with what we need to live. And as we work alongside other missionaries and see the unreached come to Christ, we gain a new family of brothers and sisters in Christ who will be a great blessing to our lives. With the sacrifices comes the great joy of seeing those in darkness rescued and adopted by God's saving grace revealed in Jesus. Though the work is tough and costly, we know that our reward is in heaven. In the midst of our labors, we must fix our gaze on the eternal life Christ has graciously given us and will lavish upon us when our work is over.

If we are going to be obedient to the Lord, we must count the cost and consider the reward. What will it cost you if God were to call you overseas? Are you willing to count the cost? It is tough, but we must be faithful to our faithful God. I was engaged to a woman during the summer of 2008, and we had to make a tough decision to break off our engagement because God was leading us in two different directions in regards to world missions. By God's grace, we counted the cost and found Christ to be more worthy than our own desires. This is an example of a small cost in the cause of missions, but what about others over the years who have endured much more for the sake of Christ?

Some of the leading pioneers in the modern missions movement had to endure much for the sake of spreading God's glory among the nations, and yet they gained much in return. William

Carey, the father of modern missions, went to India to spread the good news of Jesus. Over the years he lost three children and experienced the heartache of seeing his wife go insane on the field. He saw his first convert only after seven years of hard labor. In spite of his many afflictions, there was great reward. He translated the Bible into several Asian languages, planted many churches, established schools, and fought against social injustices of the culture, among many other things. He experienced the joy of seeing the mighty hand of God at work through Him. Hudson Taylor, missionary to China and founder of the China Inland Mission, also suffered much with the loss of his wife and four children. And yet he saw 18,000 Chinese people come to faith in Christ and helped bring in 800 missionaries to the country. Adoniram Judson, missionary to Burma, suffered the lost of three children and two wives. He spent twenty-one months in prison and experienced agonizing torture. It wasn't until his sixth year of laboring amongst the Burmese that he saw his first convert. And yet the reward he gained was the conversion of over 8,000 Burmese people and the establishment of over 100 churches. May we be inspired to count the cost and consider the reward as we look to the faithful example of others throughout history.

Preparing for a Vast Multi-Ethnic Eternity

Seeing God's heart for the nations, and His call for us to go reach them with the message of Jesus, should awaken our understanding of the vast multi-ethnic eternity that we will be a part of. This global mission is going to climax one day with the return of Jesus and all nations will be presented before Him, united as one body of joyous worshippers. "I looked, and behold, a great multitude that no one could number, from every nation, from all tribes and peoples and languages, standing before the Lamb, clothed in white robes, with palm branches in their hands, and crying out with a loud voice, 'Salvation belongs to our God who sits on the throne, and to the Lamb'" (Rev. 7:9-10).

God loves all the cultural and ethnic groups of the world. People from all cultures, ethnicities, and languages of the world will be a part of His kingdom forever. The question for us is: are we preparing for this vast multi-ethnic eternity? Do we truly love people who look and act differently than we do? Do we seek to build relationships with people of different cultures and ethnicities? Do we pray, worship, and participate in Christian community with believers of different cultures? Are we reaching out to lost people who are different than us? May we begin to live out now what will be a permanent reality when Jesus returns.

The Fuel and Goal of Missions: Worship

It is absolutely clear that God has a heart and plan for the nations, and He wants all of His followers to be a part of it. But why be a part of this mission? Obviously, it is an obedience issue, but we must ask, what is the ultimate goal of missions? What is the heartbeat and ultimate purpose of all our work? Very simply, it is the glory of God. We do missions and take part in spreading the gospel to the nations for the sake of God's glory. Our ultimate goal is that God and His Son Jesus Christ would be worshiped by people of every nation, tribe, people, and language (Rev. 7:9-10). Our ultimate aim in missions should be to see "the earth…filled with the knowledge of the glory of the Lord as the waters cover the sea" (Habakkuk 2:14). Our goal should be to see people from every tribe ascribe to the Lord the worth that is due His glorious name. Our desire should be to see the Lamb receive the reward of His suffering. And if we ourselves do not enjoy worshiping the Lord, we will not be able to strive to see Him glorified among the nations. The more we grow in worship, the more we will be motivated to see the nations come and worship.

John Piper puts it this way: "Missions is not the ultimate goal of the church. Worship is. Missions exists because worship doesn't. Worship is ultimate, not missions, because God is ultimate, not man. When this age is over, and the countless millions of the redeemed fall on their faces before the throne of God, missions will be no more. It is a temporary necessity. But worship abides forever.

"Worship, therefore, is the fuel and goal of missions. It's the goal of missions because in missions we simply aim to bring the nations into the white-hot enjoyment of God's glory. The goal of missions is the gladness of the peoples in the greatness of God. 'The Lord reigns, let the earth rejoice; let the many coastlands be glad!' (Ps. 97:1). 'Let the peoples praise you, O God; let all the peoples praise you! Let the nations be glad and sing for joy!' (Ps. 67:3-4).

"But worship is also the fuel of missions. Passion for God in worship precedes the offer of God in preaching. You can't commend what you don't cherish. Missionaries will never call out, 'Let the nations be glad!' who cannot say from the heart, 'I rejoice in the Lord….I will be glad and exult in you, I will sing your praise, O Most High' (Ps. 104:24; 9:2). Missions begins and ends in worship."[57]

A Call to Finish the Task—Go to the Unreached!

Missions exists for the glory of God. And as we have seen, missions is so important because the fullness of God's glory revealed in the coming King will not be displayed until the missionary task is complete (Matt. 24:14). The truth is we have made great progress in the last one hundred years. And the amazing thing is that many missions' experts say that we have the potential of finishing the task within this generation. "We are in the final era of pioneer missions. If we do not waver in our convictions or take our focus off the essential missionary task, we can reasonably hope to see the body

---

57 John Piper, *Let The Nations Be Glad* (Grand Rapids: Baker Academic, 1993), 17.

of Christ established and growing within the language and social structure of every people group on earth in our lifetime."[58]

Do you know what that means? That means Christ could come back very soon. Do you long for His return? Take part in finishing the task. Pray day and night for the unreached people groups. Give generously to missionaries going to the unreached people groups. Desperately inform people about the different unreached people groups in the world. Count the cost, and consider the great reward of taking the gospel to those who have never even heard the name of Jesus. This is a call for the young and old to die to themselves and embark on the greatest adventure known to man, the adventure of bringing the message of the gracious King Jesus to those who have been bound in darkness for thousands of years. This is a call to finish the task and go to the unreached so that our glorious Bridegroom and King may come and welcome us home.

58 Winter and Koch, *Perspectives*, 544.

CHAPTER 7

Pray and Fast for His Coming

Are you hungry for the return of Jesus Christ? To a large degree, the quality of your prayers and fasting will determine the answer to that question. "In prayer, real prayer, we begin to think God's thoughts after him: to desire the things he desires, to love the things he loves, to will the things he wills. Progressively, we are taught to see things from his point of view."[59] God's focus, passion, and will is to see the fullness of His glory displayed, which will begin to take place at the return of His Son, Jesus Christ. Therefore, to truly pray in accordance with the mind, heart and will of God is to pray with an intense longing for and focus on the return of Jesus. This hunger and focus on the return of Jesus is even more greatly intensified through fasting.

The Heart Behind True Prayer—Intimacy with God

Before we look at how prayer and fasting relate to the Second Coming of Jesus, it is important that we look at the true nature of prayer and fasting. Our prayers and fasting are not simply focused on the Second Coming; far from it. Though in some sense prayer and fasting are simple, there is a lot that could be said about these spiritual disciplines. But ultimately what we need to realize is that the heart

---

59 Richard Foster, *Celebration of Discipline: The Path to Spiritual Growth* (New York: Harper Collins, 1978), 33-34.

behind these disciplines is intimacy with God. The heart and soul behind true prayer is deep intimacy with our Creator and Savior.

The greatest commandment is this: "You shall love the Lord your God with all your heart and with all your soul and with all your might" (Deut. 6:5). This is why we were created. This is why we were saved. We were designed to love God with our whole being. And part of our expression of love to Him is found in our communication with Him, which is what we call prayer. Just as husbands and wives speak words of deep affection to one another, just as parents and children speak words of affirmation and trust to one another, and just as close friends share their hearts with openness and vulnerability with one another, we too are to share in this sort of intimate communication with God.

We see this close and personal communication with God in the person of Moses. "Now Moses used to take the tent and pitch it outside the camp, far off from the camp, and he called it the tent of meeting" (Ex. 33:7a). It was at this tent of meeting where people prayed and sought the Lord (v. 7b). As Moses would go out to the tent of meeting to pray, it is said that "the Lord used to speak to Moses face to face, as a man speaks to his friend" (Ex. 33:11). Moses had such an intimate life of prayer with God that it was as though he were speaking to his best friend in person. This is the heart behind true prayer. Prayer that is not fueled by deep intimacy with God is lifeless and will ultimately have no impact. Prayer first and foremost is about drawing near to God in intimacy.

The Content and Focus of Prayer

Intimacy with God should be the heart behind all of our praying. But what about the content of our prayers? What should be the specific focus of our prayers? Jesus gives us the great model prayer that shows us how we are to pray and what we are to pray for: "Our Father in heaven, hallowed by your name. Your kingdom come, your will be done, on earth as it is in heaven. Give us this day our daily bread and forgive us our debts, as we also have forgiven our debtors. And lead us not into temptation, but deliver us from evil" (Matt. 6:9-13).

Once again we see that prayer starts with intimacy with God. By calling us to address God as our Father, Jesus shows us that true prayer is about having intimacy with God. Though God is a loving father, we must come to Him realizing that He is not any ordinary father. He is our Father "in heaven." He is the holy and sovereign God who rules over the universe. As we draw near to Him with intimate love and affection, we must also bow before Him with reverence and awe. And because God is so holy and sovereign, we dare not enter His presence in our own sinful state. It is only because of Jesus' sacrificial death on the cross on our behalf that we may enter God's presence without being crushed by His wrath. By faith in Jesus and what He has done for us, we are adopted into God's family and may draw near in direct communication with our holy and loving Father.

As we draw near to God through Christ with intimacy and reverence, acknowledging the greatness and goodness of who He is, we must cry out, "hallowed be your name." In other words: "Let your name be set apart as holy. May you be honored and glorified." Jesus teaches us that the content and focus of prayer must first be that of worship. If intimacy with God is the heart behind prayer, worship is the necessary expression of that intimacy. Seeing the manifold excellencies of God's character revealed in His Word should cause our hearts to draw near to Him in worship.

As we express our worship to God in prayer, we must also ask for His glorious kingdom and His perfect will to be made manifest upon the whole earth. We are to intercede on behalf of the world and the church and pray to God that His gracious rule would cover the earth, that more and more people would be born again and brought into His kingdom, and that His just, righteous, and pure ways would be established upon the earth in the lives of His blood-bought people. Love for God in worship should overflow into love for people in intercession. Prayer is not only about personal worship and intimacy with God, it is about calling out to God for more worshippers and intimate lovers of Christ to be birthed and spread across the earth.

Another valuable aspect of prayer is to seek God's provision for our daily needs. As we come to God in intimate and reverent worship, seeking for His kingdom to spread upon the earth and His perfect will to be done, we are also called to ask God for our daily physical provision. "Give us this day our daily bread." God cares about all the needs of His children, both spiritual and physical. His love and care extends to the whole person. Therefore, we should pray for God's provision for ourselves and for all people of the world who are in need.

Without confession of our sin and prayer for deliverance from evil, we would not be able to seek God with intimacy and intercede for the world in accordance with His will. "Forgive us our debts, as we also have forgiven our debtors. And lead us not into temptation, but deliver us from evil." Sin hinders intimacy with God and our prayers of intercession. If you offend your friend, you will not be able to have a close relationship with that person until you confess your offense and see that things are made right. So it is with God. We must daily confess our sin to God and cling to the cross of Jesus for mercy. To keep our intimacy with God and love for others from being tarnished, we must also pray for God's protection and deliverance from temptation and evil of all kinds. Prayer is not only a tool for intimacy with God and impact on the world; it is also a weapon of war upon all that is evil in our lives.

In the model prayer that Jesus gave us, we see a general guideline of what the content and focus of our prayers should be. In the Apostle Paul's prayers we also see an example of what the content and focus of our prayers should look like. Let's take a look at four of his prayers:

"I do not cease to give thanks for you, remembering you in my prayers, that the God of our Lord Jesus Christ, the Father of glory, may give you a spirit of wisdom and of revelation in the knowledge of him, having the eyes of your hearts enlightened, that you may know what is the hope to which he has called you, what are the riches of his glorious inheritance in the saints, and what is the immeasurable greatness of his power toward us who believe, according to the working of his great might that he worked in Christ when he raised him from the dead and seated him at his right hand in the heavenly places, far above all rule and authority and power and dominion, and above every name that is named, not only in this age but also in the one to come. And he put all things under his feet and gave him as head over all things to the church, which is his body, the fullness of him who fills all in all" (Eph. 1:16-23).

"For this reason I bow my knees before the Father, from whom every family in heaven and on earth is named, that according to the riches of his glory he may grant you to be strengthened with power through his Spirit in your inner being, so that Christ may dwell in your hearts through faith—that you, being rooted and grounded in love, may have strength to comprehend with all the saints what is the breadth and length and height and depth, and to know the love of Christ that surpasses knowledge, that you may be filled with all the fullness of God. Now to him who is able to do far more abundantly than all that we ask or think, according to the power at work within us, to him be glory in the church and in Christ Jesus throughout all generations, forever and ever. Amen" (Eph. 3:14-21).

"And it is my prayer that your love may abound more and more, with knowledge and all discernment, so that you may approve what is excellent, and so be pure and blameless for the day of Christ, filled with the fruit of righteousness that comes through Jesus Christ, to the glory and praise of God" (Phil. 1:9-11).

"And so, from the day we heard, we have not ceased to pray for you, asking that you may be filled with the knowledge of his will in all spiritual wisdom and understanding, so as to walk in a manner worthy of the Lord, fully pleasing to him, bearing fruit in every good work and increasing in the knowledge of God. May you be strengthened with all power, according to his glorious might, for all endurance and patience with joy, giving thanks to the Father, who has qualified you to share in the inheritance of the saints in light. He has delivered us from the domain of darkness and transferred us to the kingdom of his beloved Son, in whom we have redemption, the forgiveness of sins" (Col. 1:9-14).

What can we learn from Paul's prayers? What are some of the common elements he focuses on in his different prayers? The first aspect that we notice is what was mentioned earlier: intimacy with God/worship. In the Ephesians 1 prayer, we see Paul acknowledging God for the greatness of who He is, calling Him, "the Father of glory." And what he prays for the Ephesians is that this great God, "the God of our Lord Jesus Christ, the Father of glory" would give them "a spirit of wisdom and of revelation in the knowledge of him." He prays that they would grow in a deep, intimate, heartfelt, experiential knowledge of God. The same emphasis on intimacy with God comes out in the Ephesians 3 prayer, when he prays for the believers to be rooted and grounded in the immeasurable love of Jesus. Praying for the believers to have this intimate knowledge of God is also expressed when he says, "it is my prayer that your love may abound more and more, with knowledge..." (Phil. 1:9) and that you may be "increasing in the knowledge of God" (Col. 1:10). This intimate God-glorifying drive resounds in Paul's prayers. "To him be glory in the church and in Christ Jesus throughout all generations, forever and ever" (Eph. 3:21). He prays that the believers would give "thanks to the Father" (Col. 1:12) and be filled with the "fruit of righteousness... to the glory and praise of God" (Phil. 1:11).

Another strong emphasis in Paul's prayers is the prayer for power from God. He prays that the believers would know "what is the immeasurable greatness of his power toward us who believe" (Eph. 1:19), that we would "be strengthened by his Spirit in (our) inner being" (Eph. 3:16), and that we "may...be strengthened with all power, according to his glorious might" (Col. 1:11). Too much of Christianity in the world is half-hearted, dull, stale and empty of power. We desperately need the power of God to come upon us and fill us just as we see the believers experiencing in the book of Acts. Lacking the fullness of the Holy Spirit is a tragic and prevalent problem in the church. We need to constantly be full of the power of the Holy Spirit as we pray, study and witness to this dying world.

This power that Paul prays for is also closely connected with holiness. He prays that we would "be strengthened with power through his Spirit in (our) inner being, so that Christ may dwell in (our) hearts through faith" (Eph. 3;16-17), and that we would "be strengthened with all power, according to his glorious might, for all endurance and patience with joy" (Col. 1:11). We need power to exercise faith in Christ and to endure trials with patience and joy. In other words, we need power to live holy and fruitful lives. Paul's prayers focus much on seeking after God for more holiness in the lives of believers. He prays for believers to grow in love and purity and to be filled with the fruit of righteousness (Phil. 1:9-11).

Paul's prayers are also very Christ-centered and gospel-centered. His prayer for believers to be filled with power is grounded in Christ's resurrection, ascension, and supreme Lordship (Eph. 1:19-23). Paul's prayer in Ephesians 3 is centered on the love of Jesus. His prayer for the Philippians is rooted in his thankfulness for their "partnership in the gospel" (Phil. 1:5). The closing of his prayer in Colossians 1 is an expression of thanksgiving to God for the deliverance, redemption, and forgiveness He has given us through His Son, Jesus Christ. Paul teaches us to keep the gospel central in our prayers.

Lastly, Paul also has his eyes on eternity and the Second Coming of Jesus when he prays. He prays that we would "have the eyes of (our) hearts enlightened, that (we) may know what is the hope to which he has called (us)" and "what are the riches of his glorious inheritance in the saints" (Eph. 1:18). He prays that we would be prepared for the return of Christ by living lives of purity (Phil. 1:10). He thanks God for the inheritance of future glory that we will receive (Col. 1:12). Paul teaches us that we are to pray for a greater understanding, focus, preparation and thankful anticipation for the glorious hope of the Second Coming of Jesus. This must be a key aspect of our prayer lives.

The Attitudes and Expressions of Prayer

If we want to grow in prayer, it is not only important that we understand the heart and focus of prayer, but also the attitudes and expressions of prayer. What attitudes are we to have in approaching God? What does the expression of prayer look like? In general, good communication is not just about exchanging the right content and information, but is also about how you exchange that content and information. The right attitudes, tones and expressions are key in good communication with others. For example, you could speak the most tender and romantic words in the world to your significant other, but if the words come out sounding cold and insincere, it is worthless. Using all the right words to resolve conflict with a friend will come to no avail if you come off with a harsh and proud tone. The same is true with our communication with God. How then should we approach God in prayer?

The Humility of Prayer

Scripture teaches us that we must come before God in humility. "'God opposes the proud but gives grace to the humble.' Humble yourselves, therefore, under the mighty hand of God so that at the proper time he may exalt you, casting all your anxieties on him; because he cares for you" (1 Pet. 5:5-7). Humility is inherent within the nature of true prayer. We come to God acknowledging that He is God and we are not. We are weak; He is powerful. We are dependent; He is independent. In dependence upon Him, we come before Him in prayer and cast our anxieties on Him. To come to God in prayer is to come to Him with a humble attitude.

Coming to God in humility means coming to God with trust. We cast our anxieties on Him because we know He cares for us. Like a child who humbly trusts his parents, we are to humbly trust our great Father in heaven. We are instructed from the Psalms to have this humble child-like trust: "Trust in him at all times, O people; pour out your heart before him" (Ps. 62:8). "Now I know that the Lord saves his anointed; he will answer him from his holy heaven with the saving might of his right hand. Some trust in chariots and some in horses, but we trust in the name of the Lord our God" (Ps. 20:6-7). "To you, O Lord, I lift up my soul. O my God, in you I trust" (Ps. 25:1-2). To approach God in prayer is to approach Him with a humble trust, knowing that He is our good Father. God has fulfilled all of His promises through Jesus (2 Cor. 1:20). He is a promise-keeping God, and it is by Christ and His work of salvation that we may enter His trustworthy presence in prayer.

Drawing near to our trustworthy God in humility also means drawing near to Him with reverence. "The fear of the Lord is the beginning of knowledge" (Prov. 1:7). To come to God rightly in prayer is to come to Him in reverence, knowing that He is the holy God over all. The psalmist cries out, "Tremble, O earth, at the presence of the Lord" (Ps. 114:7). Coming into the presence of God in prayer means trembling before His holiness and bowing in fearful awe of His beautifully terrifying majesty. We are to "offer to God acceptable worship, with reverence and awe, for our God is a consuming fire" (Heb. 12:28-29).

To come to God humbly is to come to God with a spirit of repentance and confession. To apologize or confess a wrong done to a person is one of the most humbling realities of life. And how much wrong have we done to God? If we would draw near to the holy God, we must humbly confess our sin and cling with faith to the Lord Jesus who died to wash away our sin. To pray to God rightly is to pray with a broken heart over our sin. "A broken and contrite heart, O God, you will not despise" (Ps. 51:17). We must be deeply troubled by our sin and filled with great sorrow over it as we come to God in true repentance. Listen to the intensity of Ezra and the people of Israel's posture before God: "While Ezra prayed and made confession, weeping and casting himself down before the house of God, a very great assembly of men, women, and children, gathered to him out of Israel, for the people wept bitterly" (Ezra 10:1). In the parable of the Pharisee and tax collector, we see the humble repentant posture of the tax collector. "The tax collector, standing far off, would not even lift up his eyes to heaven, but beat his breast, saying, 'God, be merciful to me, a sinner!'" (Luke 18:13). This is the sort of humble repentance that should be a part of the normal Christian life as we draw near to God in prayer. When was the last time you truly wept over your sin? The church has much to learn about the true nature of repentance.

The Boldness of Prayer

Though one important attitude we are to have in prayer is one of humility, this does not mean than we are to be timid or hesitant with God. In fact, the Scripture teaches us that one of the chief attitudes we are to have in prayer is boldness. We are to approach God with bold confidence. The only reason we can come to God in this way is because of Jesus. Without Jesus we dare not enter boldly into the presence of God. We would be consumed by His fierce wrath because of our sin. But because of Christ, we can draw near to God with bold confidence. "Since then we have a great high priest who has passed through the heavens, Jesus, the Son of God, let us hold fast our confession. For we do not have a high priest who is unable to sympathize with our weaknesses, but one who in every respect has been tempted as we are, yet without sin. Let us then with confidence draw near to the throne of grace, that we may receive mercy and find grace to help in time of need" (Heb. 4:14-16).

We have a mediator, the Son of God, who became a man, who lived the perfect life we did not, who died the death we deserved, who rose from the dead, ascended back to God's right hand and who is now praying for us. By faith in Him and what He has done for us, our guilt is removed, and His righteousness is charged to our account. We can now boldly and confidently draw near to God in prayer because we are clothed in the righteousness of Jesus our Savior and great High Priest.

By God's grace we now have bold access to God. We can pray to Him with bold assurance knowing that He wants us to come to Him in this way. He delights in the bold prayers of His people, and He responds well to those prayers. We see this clearly in the example of Moses. After the people of Israel heinously committed idolatry by worshiping a golden calf they had made, God says to Moses, "'I have seen this people, and behold, it is a stiff-necked people. Now therefore let me alone, that my wrath may burn hot against them and I may consume them, in order that I may make a great nation of you.' But Moses implored the Lord his God and said, 'O Lord, why does your wrath burn hot against your people, whom you have brought out of the land of Egypt with great power and with a mighty hand? Why should the Egyptians say, 'With evil intent did he bring them out, to kill them in the mountains and to consume them from the face of the earth'? Turn from your burning anger and relent from this disaster against your people. Remember Abraham, Isaac, and Israel, your servants, to whom you swore by your own self, and said to them, 'I will multiply your offspring as the stars of heaven, and all this land that I have promised I will give to your offspring, and they shall inherit it forever.' And the Lord relented from the disaster that he had spoken of bringing on his people" (Ex. 32:9-14).

Here we see Moses boldly arguing and pleading with God not to destroy the people. Filled with a passion for God's glory, he does not want the name of God to be dishonored among the Egyptians. He boldly holds onto and pleads the promises of God, and God responds by answering his request. On several other occasions Moses prayed to God in this bold way (Ex. 33:12-18; Num. 14:13-19), and this is a model for us. God delights in the bold prayers of His people because our confidence in Him and our desperation for Him to act exalt His greatness and power.

At this point, we must mention a word of caution. It is not bold prayer itself that God delights in. It is bold prayer about God-honoring things that delights God. James warns people who are selfish in their prayers and out of tune with God's will: "You ask and do not receive, because you ask wrongly, to spend it on your passions" (James 4:3). The bold prayers that God delights in and answers come from those who abide in Jesus and are therefore in tune with His will. Jesus said, "If you abide in me, and my words abide in you, ask whatever you wish, and it will be done for you" (John 15:7).

When people are dwelling in intimacy with Jesus and remaining in His Word, being in tune with God's will is the result, and bold effective prayers will follow. And part of what it means to pray with boldness is to pray with persistence. We see this bold persistence in Abraham's prayer of intercession for Sodom. As God was getting ready to destroy the wicked cities of Sodom and Gomorrah, Abraham drew near to God and said:

"'Will you indeed sweep away the righteous with the wicked? Suppose there are fifty righteous within the city? Will you then sweep away the place and not spare it for the fifty righteous who are in it? Far be it from you to do such a thing, to put the righteous to death with the wicked, so that the righteous fare as the wicked! Far be that from you! Shall not the Judge of all the earth do what is just?' And the Lord said, 'If I find at Sodom fifty righteous in the city, I will spare the whole place for their sake.' Abraham answered and said, 'Behold, I have undertaken to speak to the Lord, I who am but dust and ashes. Suppose five of the fifty righteous are lacking. Will you destroy the whole city for lack of five?' And he said, "I will not destroy it if I find forty-five there.' Again he spoke to him and said, 'Suppose forty are found there.' He answered, 'For the sake of forty I will not do it.' Then he said, 'Oh let not the Lord be angry, and I will speak. Suppose thirty are found there.' He answered, 'I will not do it, if I find thirty there.' He said, 'Behold, I have undertaken to speak to the Lord. Suppose twenty are found there.' He answered, 'For the sake of twenty I will not destroy it.' Then he said, 'Oh let not the Lord be angry, and I will speak again but this once. Suppose ten are found there.' He answered, 'For the sake of ten I will not destroy it'" (Gen. 18:22-32).

Abraham boldly clings to the justice of God, and on that basis, pleads persistently for Him not to destroy the city for the sake of a small righteous remnant. Six times he presses and pleads with God concerning this matter. Though he came to God with reverence and humility (v.27), he boldly persisted in his intercession for Sodom. This is how we are to pray.

Jesus also teaches us about the importance of persistent prayer. Jesus said to his disciples:

"Which of you who has a friend will go to him at midnight and say to him, 'Friend, lend me three loaves, for a friend of mine has arrived on a journey, and I have nothing to set before him'; and he will answer from within, 'Do not bother me; the door is now shut, and my children are with me in bed. I cannot get up and give you anything'? I tell you, though he will not get up and give him anything because he is his friend, yet because of his impudence [persistence] he will rise and give him whatever he needs. And I tell you, ask, and it will be given to you; seek, and you will find; knock, and it will be opened to you. For everyone who asks receives, and the one who seeks finds, and to the one who knocks it will be opened" (Luke 11:5-10).

Abiding in Jesus and being in tune with His will give us much warrant to pray with such bold persistence. We are to keep asking until we receive. We are to keep seeking until we find. We are to keep knocking until the door is open. As we dwell in Christ and His Word, we must be propelled into bold and persistent prayer for the things that are on God's heart. We must hold on and never let go. We must keep pressing and pleading until God comes with power and answers. God is honored by such bold persistent prayer. He is honored because it shows us how much we want Him. It shows how much we want His kingdom to come and His will to be done and He truly loves that and will answer.

Bold prayer, by nature, has an element of desperation to it. Praying with persistence means praying with desperation. And God loves when His people pray with desperation. In an event in the life of Jacob, recorded in Genesis, we see this sort of desperation in prayer to God. After stealing his brother Esau's rightful blessing from their father Isaac, years down the road on a journey back to the Promised Land, Jacob decides to send messengers to Esau to make amends. His messengers return, saying, "Esau is coming!" As Esau approaches along the path, Jacob becomes fearful. At this point, we see Jacob begin to wrestle with God.

"Jacob was left alone. And a man wrestled with him until the breaking of the day. When the man saw that he did not prevail against Jacob, he touched his hip socket, and Jacob's hip was put out of joint as he wrestled with him. Then he said, 'Let me go, for the day has broken.' But Jacob said, 'I will not let you go unless you bless me.' And he said to him, 'What is your name?' And he said, 'Jacob.' Then he said, 'Your name shall no longer be called Jacob, but Israel, for you have striven with God and with men, and have prevailed'" (Gen. 32:24-28).

Do you sense Jacob's desperation with God? Jacob wrestled with God all night until the break of day. Even after being hurt by God and being told to let go, Jacob would not. He would not let go of God until God's favor was poured out upon him. Jacob recognized his need for God's presence and God's protection as he was getting ready to face his brother Esau. With desperate persistence, he pleaded for God's blessing until he prevailed. This persistent, desperate pleading and reliance upon God honors God and is therefore rewarded.

We observe this same desperation in the barren Hannah as she pleads with the Lord for a child. The text says, "She was deeply distressed and prayed to the Lord and wept bitterly....She continued praying before the Lord" (1 Sam. 1:10, 12). She spoke to the priest saying, "I am a woman troubled in spirit...I have been pouring out my soul before the Lord" (v.15). Do you pray with this sort of desperate persistence before the Lord?

The bold persistence and desperation of prayer is not meant to be seasonal but should be a ceaseless reality in our lives. We are commanded to "pray without ceasing" (1 Thess. 5:17). Marriages die because communication ceases. Friendships are ruined because contact is lost. David says, "I will bless the Lord at all times; his praise shall continually be in my mouth" (Ps. 34:1). Our worship of God is to be continuous and our intercession for others should be ceaseless. "You who put the Lord in remembrance, take no rest, and give him no rest until he establishes Jerusalem and makes it a praise in the earth" (Isa. 62:6-7). We are to take no rest in our prayers for this lost world. We are to take no breathers in praying for the church. We are to give God no rest until He comes with power. "Keep on. Bombard God. Bombard heaven until the answers come."[60]

Another aspect of boldness in prayer to the Lord is to pray with faith. James tells us, "the prayer of faith will save the one who is sick, and the Lord will raise him up" (James 5:15). Jesus told us many times that the faith of the people was the channel by which He was pleased to heal them. It was because of their faith in His power that they were healed. Faith-filled prayers are expressions of confidence in the power of God. To pray with faith about a particular request is to pray with assurance and confidence that God will answer that prayer. All prayers should have an element of faith that He will answer in His particular way. There will be times when we are unsure of His will. At that point, we will be called to pray simply believing He will know best how to answer. Other times, we will have insight through the Holy Spirit to believe more assuredly that God will answer in a specific way, for example, a prayer for healing.

But just because we have a strong desire for something and decide to work up faith that God will give it to us, does not mean He will. That is false and manipulative faith. True faith-filled prayers come from being intimately in tune with God's will by abiding in Jesus and His Word (John 15:7). Knowing His Word, His revealed will, is key. The more we abide in His Word, the more we will know His will, and therefore, the more we will be able to pray with expectation and confidence in the power of God. For those who abide in Jesus and His Word, the promise of Christ applies: "...Whatever you ask in prayer, believe that you

---

60 Martyn Lloyd-Jones, *Revival*, 261.

have received it, and it will be yours" (Mark 11:24). Thus, praying with expectant faith is an expression of bold prayer.

To pray with boldness at times also involves engaging in spiritual warfare. War is fierce and intense. War is about fighting, contending and destroying. As Christians, we are soldiers of Christ who are enlisted in an epic spiritual war for the ages. There is an enemy to fight. "We do not wrestle against flesh and blood, but against the rulers, against the authorities, against the cosmic powers over this present darkness, against the spiritual forces of evil in the heavenly places" (Eph. 6:12). The devil and his demons are out to steal, kill, and destroy (John 10:10). They are out to lead people away from Christ. At Jesus' death on the cross He gained victory over the devil and his powers (Col. 2:15), but the complete consummation of that victory will not come to pass until the end. So there is still a battle we are engaged in. We have many weapons in our warfare, but prayer is most certainly a significant one. In the context of instructing us to put on the whole armor of God, Paul tells us that we are to "(pray) at all times in the Spirit, with all prayer and supplication" (Eph. 6:18).

Prayer involves waging war. Prayer involves calling upon our great Commander and Chief for victory and deliverance from evil. David said, "The Lord is my rock and my fortress and my deliverer, my God, my rock, in whom I take refuge, my shield, and the horn of my salvation, my stronghold. I call upon the Lord, who is worthy to be praised, and I am saved from my enemies" (Ps. 18:2-3). Like David, Jesus instructs His followers to call upon God for deliverance from enemies. When the disciples failed to cast out a demon and asked Jesus why, Jesus said to them, "This kind cannot be driven out by anything but prayer" (Mark 9:29). Driving out demons involves waging war through the power of prayer. We are called to take the authority we have in Christ and wage war upon the enemy when confronted with his schemes.

Not only do we have an enemy on the outside, but also on the inside. In this spiritual war we face, we must wrestle against the temptations and attacks of demonic powers, as well as, our own inward sinful impulses. The devil is not our only concern. Our own sinful nature is waging war against us on a daily basis. The selfishness, pride, and lust of our own hearts are seeking to kill our love for the Lord. We are commanded to put to death our fleshly desires by the Spirit's power (Rom. 8:13). We must pray for God's grace and power to fight sin and to put it to death in our lives. We are in a ruthless war, and prayer is our direct line of communication with our Great Commander who holds the victory in His hands. To pray with boldness involves engaging in intense spiritual war.

The Attentiveness of Prayer

Have you ever had a conversation with someone that you knew was not listening to you? It's frustrating, isn't it? How do you think God feels? It is a good thing that God is patient with His children because the sad truth is that many times we do not listen to God when we pray. We are not attentive to His Spirit's leading. We just go babbling on with our requests and do not keep our spiritual ear open to His Spirit. It's more like a one-way conversation rather than the normal two-way kind. Since when did normal, healthy relationships consist of one person talking and the other listening all the time? It is obviously true that God has spoken through His Word and we are to listen to it, but it is also true that God speaks to us and leads us in prayer.

We are meant to always be attentive to God's Spirit in our praying. "…Without it our praying is vain repetition (Matt. 6:7). Listening to the Lord is the first thing, the second thing, and the third thing necessary for successful intercession."[61]   We see this attentive posture to God in prayer throughout Scripture. Samuel, the judge and prophet of Israel, was displeased when the people of Israel demanded him to appoint them a king (1 Sam. 8:6). But we are told, "Samuel prayed to the Lord. And the Lord said to Samuel, 'Obey the voice of the people in all that they say to you, for they have not rejected you, but they have rejected me from being king over them'" (1 Sam. 8:6-7). Samuel could have easily let his own desire and displeasure determine how he would respond to the people, but instead he attentively prayed to the Lord, and God responded by giving him direction on what to do.

In the life of Jesus, we also see an example of someone who listened to God when he prayed. "In these days he went out to the mountain to pray, and all night he continued in prayer to God. And when day came, he called his disciples and chose from them twelve, whom he named apostles" (Luke 6:12-13). It was through talking to and listening to God in prayer that He discovered the guidance He needed concerning who He would choose to be His apostles. He was attentive to the Father's voice and will. We see another example of this attentiveness towards God in Acts 13:1-3. "Now there were in the church at Antioch prophets and teachers, Barnabas, Simeon who was called Niger, Lucius of Cyrene, Manaen a member of the court of Herod the tetrarch, and Saul. While they were worshipping the Lord and fasting, the Holy Spirit said, 'Set apart for me Barnabas and Saul for the work to which I have called them.' Then after fasting and praying they laid their hands on them and sent them off."

It was during a time of worship, prayer and fasting that the Holy Spirit directed the church to send off Barnabas and Saul as missionaries to the Gentiles. During a time of desperate seeking

---

61 Foster, *Celebration of Discipline*, 39.

and hungering for God, He gave direction that would prove to be monumental in the history of the church. This shows how important it is to be open, vulnerable and attentive before the Lord. If we are to connect with the heart and will of God, we must cultivate a stillness and attentiveness as we pray.

Word-Driven Prayer

Attentiveness in prayer relates directly to being driven by God's Word as we pray. It is those who abide in intimacy with Jesus and who have His Words abiding in them, that will be attentive to God and therefore have an effective prayer life (John 15:7). To pray successfully in tune with God, we must have our minds and hearts saturated with the Word of God. "If the Word of God abides in you, you can pray because you meet the great God with His own words and thus overcome omnipotence with omnipotence. You put your finger down upon the very lines and say, 'Do as You have said.' This is the best praying in all the world. So be filled with God's Word. Study what Jesus has said, what the Holy Ghost has left on record in this divinely inspired book, and in proportion as you feed on, retain and obey the Word in your life, you will be a master in the art of prayer."[62] Prayers that honor God will be those that are driven and saturated with His Word.

Spirit-Empowered Prayer

It is not enough, though, to just know the Word and pray it. The devil knows the Word better than any of us and can recite it well to God. The question is: how are we using the Word in our prayers? How is the Word shaping, softening and directing our hearts? There is a lot in the Bible. One Scripture might be better

62 Charles Spurgeon, *The Power of Prayer in the Believer's Life*, ed. Robert Hall (Lynnwood, WA: Emerald Books, 1993), 41.

to pray in a certain time and context of prayer than another. So what is there to be said about this matter?

What this shows us is that we need the Word and Spirit working together in our prayers. In our prayers, we must be both Word-driven and Spirit-empowered. "Likewise the Spirit helps us in our weakness. For we do not know what to pray for as we ought, but the Spirit himself intercedes for us with groanings too deep for words" (Rom. 8:26-27). We are told to "(pray) at all times in the Spirit" (Eph. 6:18). Jude 20 says, "But you, beloved, building yourselves up in your most holy faith and praying in the Holy Spirit…" The bland and dry formality of many Christians' prayers has just got to go. True prayer must be guided by and full of the Holy Spirit's activity. We have no clue what to pray for without God's Spirit. True prayer must be full of the Holy Spirit's deep groanings within us. Before we so quickly start babbling off vain repetitious prayers, we need to learn to take a deep breath, pause, pray for the Spirit's guidance, and listen as we call out to God. I am not suggesting that every time we pray we have to wait and ask for the Spirit's guidance. I am merely pointing out that we need to be more aware and attentive to the Spirit's groanings upon our hearts as we pray. The body of Christ desperately needs to learn more about what it means to pray empowered by the Spirit.

Holiness-conditioned Prayer

Effective Spirit-empowered prayer comes from a heart and life transformed by the Spirit. The healthiness of one's prayers will be determined by the holiness of one's life. This connection between healthy prayer and holy living is addressed in several Scriptures. "The end of all things is at hand; therefore be self-controlled and sober-minded for the sake of your prayers" (1 Pet. 4:7). The way we live and think will either have a good or bad effect on our prayer lives. Peter tells us that if a husband does not love and honor his wife, his prayers will be hindered. "Husbands, live with your wives in an understanding way, showing honor to the woman as the weaker vessel, since they are heirs with you of the grace of life, so that your prayers may not be hindered" (1 Pet. 3:7).

Have you ever deeply offended your spouse, a friend, or a co-worker? What was the result? Communication probably became broken, distant and cold. Maybe they gave you the silent treatment or walked away from you to get some space. Our behavior effects our communication with one another. It is the same way with God. Our sin separates us from intimate communication with Him. It is true that God listens to the lost sinner's cry for mercy and gives him access into His presence through Christ's work of salvation. It is true that He hears and answers the prayers of His imperfect people. But there is a sense in which our sin, especially habitual and un-repentant sin, can hinder our communication with the Lord. That is part of the reason why we must strive after holiness by His grace. We must remember "the prayer of the upright is acceptable to him" (Prov. 15:8) and "the prayer of the righteous has great power as it is working" (James 5:16). "...Whatever we ask we receive from him, because we keep his commandments and do what pleases him" (1 John 3:22). To have a healthy and powerful prayer life, we must be walking in holiness by His grace.

The Importance of United Prayer

The Christian life is not a solo pursuit. It is not just about me and God, but *us and God*. Prayer is not simply a conversation between the individual and God but is meant to be a conversation between the church and God. Because the church is one body of believers, we should expect and strive to be one in prayer. "I appeal to you, brothers, by our Lord Jesus Christ and by the love of the Spirit, to strive together with me in your prayers to God on my behalf" (Rom. 15:30). Togetherness in prayer cannot be emphasized enough. This is the way basic Christianity is supposed to be.

In times of desperation and repentance, the people of God in the Old Testament would gather together to seek the Lord (2 Chron. 20:1-4, Ezra 10:1, Neh. 9:1-3, Joel 2:13-16). In times of worship and celebration they would also assemble together (Lev. 23). In the early church community, we again see this together-ness in the believers' devotion to the Lord (Acts 2:42-47). United prayer is one important aspect of this togetherness in the Chris-tian community. As the believers were gathered together waiting for the Holy Spirit to come, it says, "All these with one accord were devoting themselves to prayer…" (Acts 1:14). They were all gathered together in the same place, praying. They were united in one accord, seeking the face of the Lord. This is an extremely important point to make because just shortly after that the out-pouring of the Holy Spirit came on Pentecost. United corporate prayer was a definite factor in the outpouring of the Holy Spirit.

What we see here is that God loves to answer the united prayers of His people. It is like a father whose child comes and begs him to take him to the park. The father says no. Then all five of his children come to him begging, "Daddy, please take us to the park. Please. Please. Please, Daddy!" At that point, the father agrees and takes them to the park. God answers the united prayers of His people. Yes, he obviously answers the prayers of individuals, but history shows that many great outpourings of His Spirit took place when multiple believers were gathered together in prayer. This sense of united corporate prayer is something we have lost in the Christian church, and we must regain it for the sake of God's glory.

Prayer and the End Times

Prayer is an enormous topic that cannot be covered here ex-tensively. But I wanted us to at least take a look at the heart behind prayer, the content and focus of prayer, and some of the attitudes and expressions of prayer. Because prayer is an important aspect of the Christian faith, preparation for the Lord Jesus' return will involve learning what it means to truly pray. But more specifically we must ask, how does prayer relate to the Second Coming?

In Luke 18, we see Jesus teaching His followers about persistent prayer; particularly in the context of the end times. After giving a parable to teach us about persistent prayer, he says, "And will not God give justice to his elect, who cry to him day and night? Will he delay long over them? I tell you, he will give justice to them speedily. Nevertheless, when the Son of Man comes, will he find faith on earth?" (Luke 18:7-8).

God's people are to pray with persistence, longing and crying out for God to vindicate them and finally make all things right. God will bring this about when Jesus returns to the earth. Because many will fall away and the love of many will grow cold (Matt. 24:10, 12), we must "stay awake at all times, praying that [we] may have strength to escape all these things that are going to take place" (Luke 21:36). Jesus teaches us that we are to pray with persistence and watchfulness as we anticipate His return.

One of the requests that the Lord Jesus taught us to ask of the Father was, "your kingdom come." When we pray for God's kingdom to come, this should always include praying for it to come in all its fullness. We are not just to pray for pockets of the world to be full of God's glory and grace, we are to pray for the day when the whole earth will be covered with the knowledge of the glory of the Lord as the waters cover the sea (Hab. 2:14). We are not just to pray for God's kingdom to come upon our workplaces, schools, and families, but we are to pray for the day the Lord Jesus comes and brings the fullness of the kingdom upon the whole earth.

The amazing and mysterious truth is that the prayers of the church help usher in the consummation of human history and the final fulfillment of God's purposes. As Jesus gets ready to open the scroll of human history and the final outpourings of God's judgment, we see the twenty-four elders and the four living creatures bowing down before Him, "each holding a harp, and golden bowls full of incense, which are the prayers of the saints" (Rev. 5:8). In the context of the end times and God's final judgments, we see the prayers of the saints somehow involved and playing a part. We see this again in chapter 8:

> "When the Lamb opened the seventh seal, there was silence in heaven for about half an hour. Then I saw the seven angels who stand before God, and seven trumpets were given to them. And another angel came and stood at the altar with a golden censer, and he was given much incense to offer with the prayers of all the saints on the golden altar before the throne, and the smoke of the incense, with the prayers of the saints, rose before God from the hand of the angel. Then the angel took the censer and filled it with fire from the altar and threw it on the earth, and there were peals of thunder, rumblings, flashes of lightning, and an earthquake" (Rev. 8:1-5).

Here we see the prayers of the saints rising and accumulating before God, resulting in fiery judgments being poured down upon the earth. God's people are to pray for the fullness of His kingdom to come and for His final purposes to be done. One day He will answer. Our prayers play a significant role in the final judgments of God and the ushering in of Christ's eternal kingdom. Think about how amazing that is! Never underestimate the power and importance of prayer!

What we have seen is that prayer is extremely important in relation to the end times. The prayers of the saints will be one of the great means through which our great King returns. If this does not give you motivation to pray, I do not know what will. Ultimately, the prayer of our hearts should be that of the final chapter of Revelation, "Come, Lord Jesus!" (Rev. 22:20). Every prayer should be filled with a desperate ache for Him to come back soon. With deep groanings within, we should cry out with all our hearts, "Come, Lord Jesus!" Do you miss Him that badly?

Things to Pray for in Relation to Christ's Return

Scripture makes it clear that we should long for and pray desperately for Jesus to return. But in order for Him to return, certain things must take place first. Before He comes, His Bride must be prepared and ready for His return (Rev. 19:7). It is true that many within the visible church will fall away in those times (Matt. 24:10), but those who are His true people will endure till the end (Matt. 24:13). He will pour out His Spirit and make sure of that. "And in the last days it shall be, God declares, that I will pour out my Spirit on all flesh..." (Acts 2:17). It is true that at Pentecost this prophecy from Joel had a partial fulfillment and that the last days began to be ushered in, in a certain sense. But keeping in line with the "already but not yet" principle of prophecy we see in Scripture, I believe it is clear that there will be a greater fulfillment of this prophecy before Jesus returns (vs. 19-20). There will come a time of a great outpouring of the Holy Spirit before Christ returns. The true church will be revived and a harvest of salvation will come to the lost (v. 21).

I believe it is extremely important that we begin now in praying for revival for the church worldwide. But what does it mean to prayer for revival? "The prayer for revival is, ultimately, a prayer based upon a concern for the manifestation of the glory of God."[63] What we are to pray for concerning revival in the church is that God would pour out His Spirit and show us the depths of His glory. It is a prayer for God to reveal the supreme weight of His holiness and power to the hearts of His people. It is a prayer for God to display the overwhelming beauty of His grace revealed in the gospel of Jesus to the souls of His people. It is a prayer for the church to be humbled, purified, emboldened, and set on fire with passion for God. It is a prayer for the fear of the Lord to grip members of the church and for inexpressible joy to fill their hearts. It is a prayer for the power of God to come. The things Paul prayed for the church in Ephesus (Eph. 1:16-23, 3:14-21), should be the constant prayers of our heart for the church world-wide. We must pray for this sort of revival so that the Bride of Christ may be prepared for our beautiful Bridegroom's return. Are you desperately praying for revival?

Before Jesus returns, we also know that the Great Commission must be finished (Matt. 24:14). All of the unreached people groups of the world must be reached with the gospel. Therefore, we are to pray diligently for this task to be completed. Jesus said, "The harvest is plentiful, but the laborers are few; therefore pray earnestly to the Lord of the harvest to send out laborers into his harvest" (Matt. 9:37-38). We must pray night and day that more workers would be sent into the unreached harvest fields. We must pray for the kingdom of God to come upon all the people groups of the world. We must pray for salvation to come and disciples to be made in every remaining people group. We must pray for gospel-centered churches to be planted and reproduced. We must pray for human trafficking victims to be rescued, for orphans to find homes, for the hungry to be fed, and for the grace of God re-

---

63 Martyn Lloyd-Jones, *Revival*, 216.

vealed in the death and resurrection of Jesus to reach the darkest places on earth. Are you praying for the unreached harvest fields with desperate longing for Jesus' return?

Not only must the unreached nations be reached before Christ returns, but Israel must be saved and brought back into the covenant. "Lest you be wise in your own conceits, I want you to understand this mystery, brothers: a partial hardening has come upon Israel, until the fullness of the Gentiles has come in. And in this way all Israel will be saved" (Rom. 11:25-26). God's covenant was originally with Israel but once the Messiah came, for the most part they rejected Him and were broken off from the covenant. There has been a hardening of the hearts of Israelites down through the centuries, during which the Gentiles have been flooding into the covenant with God through Christ. But one day, we are told, "all Israel will be saved." Now I do not believe this means every ethnic Jew will come to Christ during the time before Christ returns, but I do believe it means there will be a massive conversion of the Jews who turn from their sins and put their faith in Jesus as the Messiah. Therefore, we should be praying for God to save the Israelites. "Brothers, my heart's desire and prayer to God for them (Israel) is that they may be saved" (Rom. 10:1). The amazing reality is that more Jews have been coming to Christ in the last few decades than ever before. We must pray for Israel.

Prayer + Fasting = Intensified Hunger for God and the Coming of Jesus

If there is one spiritual discipline that I rarely hear Christians talking about it is fasting. Maybe that is because we do not hear teaching about fasting and are unsure of what it means exactly and how much value it can bring to the Christian life. Or maybe we are just too addicted to food and overrun by our culture's over-consumption. It is probably a mixed bag. There are many different places we could go in Scripture to learn about fasting, but let us take a look at Acts 13:2-3. After names of people in the church at Antioch are mentioned, it says, "While they were worshipping the Lord and fasting, the Holy Spirit said, 'Set apart for me Barnabas and Saul for the work to which I have called them.' Then after fasting and praying they laid their hands on them and sent them off."

First, we must notice what it is the believers were doing. It says they were worshipping, fasting and praying. These three are connected. Ultimately, what we see here is that the people were seeking hard after God. And part of what it means to seek hard after God is to fast from food. To intensely pursue God is to go without food at times, with a heart fixed on God, to symbolize and express our deep hunger for God. "It's a physical exclamation point at the end of the sentence, 'We hunger for you, O God, to come in power.' It's a cry with our body, not just our soul: 'I really mean it, Lord! This much, I hunger for you. I want the manifestation of Your presence more than I want food."[64]

Another point to consider in this incident in Acts 13 is that during this time of worship, fasting and prayer, God gave them specific guidance concerning the commissioning of missionaries from the church. Fasting combined with prayer helps make special room for us to be more attentive to God's leading in our lives. And what we see here is that God lead His people into a great mission that would change the world forever. It is important to see here that fasting and prayer is connected to missions. By implication, what this tells us is that fasting should be connected to our prayers for the leading of God's people into mission across the world. When we pray for revival in the church, for the unreached mission field and for the people of Israel, we also should combine these prayers with fasting, thus expressing our intense hunger for God's will and work to be done.

---

64 John Piper, *A Hunger for God* (Wheaton, IL: Crossway Books, 1997), 110.

Not only is fasting an expression of hunger and longing for God and for God's will to be done, it is also more specifically an expression of longing for the Messiah to come. We see this in the example of Anna in Luke 2:36-38:

> "And there was a prophetess, Anna, the daughter of Phanuel, of the tribe of Asher. She was advanced in years, having lived with her husband seven years from when she was a virgin, and then as a widow until she was eighty-four. She did not depart from the temple, worshipping with fasting and prayer night and day. And coming up at that very hour she began to give thanks to God and to speak of him (the Messiah) to all who were waiting for the redemption of Jerusalem."

This prophetess, Anna, was constantly in the temple worshipping, fasting and praying, at least for sixty years. Verse 38 infers that her fasting and praying were specifically connected with a longing for the Messiah. She fasted and prayed day and night, decade after decade, in worship to God, hungering and longing for the Messiah to come and bring redemption.

The question should then be: do we have that sort of intense longing for the Messiah's Second Coming? When the people asked Jesus why his disciples did not fast, "Jesus said to them, 'Can the wedding guests fast while the bridegroom is with them? As long as they have the bridegroom with them, they cannot fast. The days will come when the bridegroom is taken away from them, and then they will fast in that day" (Mark 2:19-20). Fasting in the Old Testament was usually an expression of great mourning and gloominess. Jesus is saying, "Look, weddings are not supposed to be gloomy and sad. When the Bridegroom is present, there should be great joy and celebration. It should be a party. Since I, the Bridegroom am here, it's time to celebrate. But one day I will leave and then the people will fast again."

It was not time for the people to fast. It was time for the people to feast. The Bridegroom, the gracious lover of mankind, was in their midst. But one day He would be taken away, and then fasting would begin again. The Bridegroom has now been taken away from us, but He is coming back again in all of His beauty and glory. We are now to fast as an expression of deep longing and hunger for His return. The fullness of our satisfaction in the beloved Bridegroom has not yet come; therefore, we are to fast with great hunger for Him to return quickly.

An Exhortation: Pray and Fast for His Coming

For the church to be ready for the return of Jesus, she must learn the true nature of prayer and fasting. The new heavens and the new earth will be a place of intimate communication with and never-ending satisfaction in our triune God. To prepare for eternity, we must learn to intimately communicate with and hunger for God now. That is why prayer and fasting are so important. It is through the weak means of His praying and fasting people that God will do great works among the nations and manifest the fullness of His glory. It is through the prayers and fasting of His people that He will send His Son Jesus to the earth to make all things new. Are you growing in the mighty work of prayer? Do you fast in longing for the return of Jesus? The sad thing is: "The absence of fasting is the measure of our contentment with the absence of Christ."[65] Let us not be content with His absence. May God fill our hearts with His grace, may He open our lips in prayer and may He cause us to empty our stomachs of food at times, as we desperately long for the return of our precious Bridegroom, Jesus.

---

65 Ibid, 93.

CHAPTER 8

Sticking Together as the Day Draws Near

If the Christian life could be compared to a sport, it would be similar to basketball, soccer or football. Unlike golf or tennis, the Christian life is a team effort. Christianity is not an individualistic pursuit or endeavor. It is about being committed to others and working with others in pursuit of God's glory. This book would be a failure if it gave people the impression that we can heed the exhortations of Scripture and prepare for Christ's return on our own as individuals. This simply is not the case. We need each other. We need the local church.

The Local Church and the End Times

Through Jesus and His saving work on the cross, we now have direct access to God and can draw near to Him by faith in what Christ has done for us. In light of this truth, the writer of Hebrews exhorts us to hold tight to this reality, especially in the context of the local church. "Let us hold fast the confession of our hope without wavering, for he who promised is faithful. And let us consider how to stir up one another to love and good works, not neglecting to meet together, as is the habit of some, but encouraging one another, and all the more as you see the Day drawing near" (Heb. 10:23–25).

To be a Christian means to trust in Christ and what He has done and to continue in that trust without wavering. The evidence that one truly is a Christian is that the person will be pressing forward in faith, loving God and others, and doing good works to the glory of God. The truth we see here, though, is that we as believers need to be stirring up and motivating each other in these realities. We need help from the body of Christ if we are going to continue pressing forward in the Christian life. That is why it says we are not to neglect meeting together, as is the habit of some. We need the local church. We need to be committed to a local body of believers so that we can find and give the encouragement we need to keep going and growing in the Christian life.

Notice specifically what he references in this exhortation. We are not to neglect to meet together, as is the habit of some, but we are to "(encourage) one another, and all the more as (we) see the Day drawing near" (v.25). As Christians, we are to be committed to a local body of believers that we will meet with in order to be nourished and encouraged in the Christian life. And we are especially to do this as we see the day of Christ's return drawing nearer and nearer.

In light of the Second Coming of Jesus, we are exhorted to be committed to a local church. In order for us as Christians to be prepared for Christ's return, we must continually be receiving and giving nourishment in the context of the local church. As the days grow darker and the times get harder, we will need the local church more than ever. As the days of great deception, ungodliness, and persecution draw near, we will need fellow Christians more than ever. For us to endure those final days and be ready to see our glorious King face to face, we must stick together.

The Life of the Local church

From this passage in Hebrews, we see that the local church is extremely valuable and is required for all true Christians. But what is the local church all about? What should the life of the local church look like? I think we see one of the clearest pictures of what the local church should look like in Acts 2:42-47.

"And they devoted themselves to the apostles' teaching and fellowship, to the breaking of bread and the prayers. And awe came upon every soul, and many wonders and signs were being done through the apostles. And all who believed were together and had all things in common. And they were selling their possessions and belongings and distributing the proceeds to all, as any had need. And day by day, attending the temple together and breaking bread in their homes, they received their food with glad and generous hearts, praising God and having favor with all the people. And the Lord added to their number day by day those who were being saved."

Fellowship

In this passage we see the word "fellowship" as part of the description of this early church community. This word means to share or participate. It means to hold something in common. Here in this early church community, we see a strong sense of togetherness, closeness, and unity. Fellowship means more than just hanging out with people. "First, it expresses what we share in together (our common inheritance); second, what we share out together (our common service); and third, what we share with each other (our mutual responsibility)."[66] It expresses the heart and depth of what true community should be. And it is this sort of deep commonality and togetherness that should be a part of the life of every local church, something which is lacking in many churches today.

Centered on Truth

The early church community was not a community just for the sake of "community" which seems to be the buzzword these

---

66 John Stott, *The Living Church* (Downers Grove, IL: InterVarsity Press, 2007), 90.

days in our postmodern culture. Everybody is longing for authentic community, a place where they can belong. And yet many times community is spoken of with this sort of undefined vagueness. This was not the case with this early church community. Their fellowship, their community, was centered on truth. It was a community centered on specific teaching, and this teaching defined who and what this community would be. "And they devoted themselves to the apostles' teaching."

The apostles' teaching refers to the teachings of Jesus passed down to the apostles. It would refer to all the things Jesus taught. At the heart and center of His teachings would be the good news of His perfect life, death, and resurrection for sinners. The gospel message as seen in the book of Acts was the central message of the early church community. The centrality of the gospel is clearly seen in the reference to "the breaking of bread" which refers to the Lord's Supper, symbolizing Jesus' great work of salvation on our behalf. The gospel was indeed the central and defining truth of the early church.

More broadly speaking, being devoted to the apostles' teaching meant being devoted to the Word of God as a whole, seeing that the apostles did have divine authority in writing the New Testament Scriptures. It was Paul who said "I did not shrink from declaring to you the whole council of God" (Acts 20:27). The foundation of the early church community was the whole of God's perfect and trustworthy Word. This community was centered on the Scriptures.

And it was the preaching of these Scriptures that took front and center in the life of the early church. The importance of the preaching of God's Word is clearly shown in Paul's charge to Timothy: "I charge you in the presence of God and of Christ Jesus, who is to judge the living and the dead, and by his appearing and his kingdom: preach the word; be ready in season and out of season; reprove, rebuke, and exhort, with complete patience and teaching"

(2 Tim. 4:1-2). Paul uses strong words in the giving of this mighty charge for Timothy to preach God's Word. This highlights its extreme importance in the life of the local church and the desperate need we have for hearing the preaching of God's Word.

Sadly, many in today's church do not value the preaching of God's Word and look at it as an outdated form of communication. As the peculiar people of God, however, we must remember not to rely on man's wisdom or the culture's insight into effective communication, but on God's counter intuitive wisdom and perfect insight in how to communicate to His world. What we need to realize is that this issue is not a matter of preference, but of obedience. "Preach the Word!" That simple imperative frames the act of preaching as an act of obedience, and that is where any theology of preaching must begin. Preaching did not emerge from the church's experimentation with communication techniques. The church does not preach because preaching is thought to be a good idea or an effective technique. The sermon has not earned its place in Christian worship by proving its utility in comparison with other means of communication or aspects of worship. Rather, we preach because we have been commanded to preach. Preaching is a commission—a charge. As Paul boldly stated, it is the task of the minister of the gospel to "'preach the word...in season and out of season' (2 Timothy 4:2). A theology of preaching begins with the humble acknowledgment that preaching is not a human invention but a gracious creation of God and a central part of His revealed will for the church."[67]

Though many factors are involved, the lack of appetite for hearing God's Word preached partly has to do with the fact that many churches do not practice biblical preaching. To preach biblically is to be true to the text of Scripture by not putting one's own

---

67 R. Albert Mohler, Jr., *He Is Not Silent: Preaching In A Postmodern World* (Chicago, IL: Moody Publishers, 2008), 39.

meaning into it, but by bringing out the meaning that is already there and was originally intended. It is to break down and explain the meaning of the Scriptures in their proper context and to apply it rightly. This is what is called "expository preaching." And it is this sort of preaching that is lacking in many churches today.

True biblical preaching is not only about explaining the text but also has to do with how one delivers the text. "Preaching is declaring the Word of God to men…The job of the preacher is to declare it and to do so in a way that demands a response."[68] Preaching involves reproving, rebuking, and exhorting. To preach is to passionately and confidently speak God's Word and call man to respond appropriately. To preach God's Word as God's Spirit-empowered messenger is to speak with authority.

This authoritative deliverance of God's Word is lacking when the church gives up biblical preaching in exchange for entertainment-based and culturally inoffensive ways of com-munication. The Church desperately needs Spirit-empowered preachers who will declare the Word of God and the gospel of grace with radical boldness and authority. "Any study of church history, and particularly any study of the great periods of revival or reawakening, demonstrates above everything else just this one fact: that the Christian Church during all such periods has spoken with authority. The great characteristic of all revivals has been the authority of the preacher. There seemed to be some-thing new, extra, and irresistible in what he declared on behalf of God."[69] The sad truth is that the Church has been stripped bare of true power from God. We have conformed to the world and settled merely for the non-offensive cozy dialogue that our culture so highly praises.

---

68 Stephen McQuoid, *The Beginner's Guide to Expository Preaching* (UK: Christian Focus Publications, Ltd., 2002), 35-36.
69 Martyn Lloyd Jones, *Authority* (Downers Grove, IL: InterVarsity Press, 1958), 10.

Where are all the radical gospel-centered preachers who have enough bold love to go against the grain of our anti-authority driven culture and give people what they truly need, the life transforming power of the Word of God? May God begin to raise these sorts of preachers up in our churches and on our streets for His glory.

Prayer

The local church community is not only a people of truth but also a people of prayer. Acts 2:42 says they devoted themselves "to the prayers." God's people are a praying people. As the people of God receive the truth of God, they must engage with and respond to God in prayer. The local church should be a tangible and visible demonstration of what it means to have direct and intimate communication with God. Prayer in the local church is about the family of God coming together to seek the face of our heavenly Father.

Do our local churches know what it means to be devoted to prayer like the early church was? Are our churches so caught up in programs and planning that little emphasis is put upon prayer? Charles Spurgeon, the great Baptist preacher of the 19th century, pointing people to the basement of the church where people were praying continually, would say, "Here is the powerhouse of this church."

The Power of God

There is power in prayer, even in the prayers of just one Christian (James 5:16b). And yet how much more of God's power will be displayed when the people of God come together to pray? Acts 2:43 states, "And awe came upon every soul, and many wonders and signs were being done through the apostles." The local church should be a place where the power of God manifests itself to a watching world. God is all about displaying the greatness of

His power and glory to the whole world. It is through His church, His people, that He chooses to do it.

Signs and wonders are meant to bear witness to the power of the gospel (Acts 14:3). Miracles, healings and signs and wonders, done for the glory of Christ and by the power of the Holy Spirit, are highly valuable, deeply impactful to the lost world and can be a great blessing when pursued rightly.

Love and Generosity

Truth and power without love is not very compelling or attractive. Therefore, it is important to understand love as the key expression and outworking of life in the local church. "And all who believed were together and had all things in common. And they were selling their possessions and belongings and distributing the proceeds to all, as any had need" (vs. 44-45). Love expressed in unity and generosity should be the mark of every true local church. Love for one another and generosity towards those in need mark the signs of a healthy body of believers. And it truly is encouraging to see this reality in action. Whether it is raising funds for a friend going on a short-term mission trip, helping cover the rent of a man who was just laid off from his job or providing meals for one who cannot get around well due to a recent surgery, all these are examples of expressions of love and generosity that should be on display in the local church. Jesus indeed said, "By this all people will know that you are my disciples, if you have love for one another" (John 13:35).

Worship

Ultimately, the heart and focus behind this community of truth and love is God Himself. What drives the church is a passion to glorify God for all that He is and has done through His Son Jesus Christ. The local church community is a community of worship-

pers, first and foremost. "And day by day, attending the temple together and breaking bread in their homes, they received their food
with glad and generous hearts, praising God…" (vs. 46-47a). The
local church is about bringing praise and worship to the almighty
God. What does it mean to truly worship? Worship is a joyful and
reverent, God-centered, Christ-exalting disposition of the heart,
informed by the mind's knowledge of Scripture, which spills out
into words and actions that ascribe worth and value to God. This
is what it truly means to worship. The local church community
is a community that ascribes worth to God through song, prayer,
preaching and day to day lives of love and thanksgiving.

Witness

How could the church really be the church if it only looked to
the inside and not to the outside? We are meant to be salt and light
to the world. It is not enough to be worshippers of God together
with the local church; we are to go out and bring in more worshippers of God. Acts 2:47 says the early church was "…praising God
and having favor with all the people. And the Lord added to their
number day by day those who were being saved." We are to be witnesses to this lost and dying world. The local church community
is not a social club but is about being equipped to go out into the
world to speak the good news of Jesus with all who will hear it.
We bear a message that God is holy and that mankind is sinful and
desperately lost. Jesus Christ, the God-man, who died for man's
rebellion and rose again, is the only Savior, and without trusting in
Him mankind will be justly punished forever. With Him is forgiveness of sins and eternal life with the perfect loving God. We must
go out into our schools, workplaces, communities and even to the
nations, to serve with compassion and to speak with boldness this
great message of grace beyond compare. A church that is not a witnessing church is a dying church.

The Leadership of the Local church

For the local church to function properly and to live in the realities to which the Scriptures call us, there must be leadership and structure. And not just any sort of leadership will do, but only what God has appointed in His Word (Eph. 4:11-13, 1 Tim. 3:1-13).[70] When many think of church leadership they think of the senior pastor who is in charge. The pastor is the one who preaches, teaches and leads God's people to growth in Christ-likeness. It is true from Scripture that we see this church office of pastor, also described in synonymous terms as elder, overseer, or bishop.

The Plurality of Elders

Where many churches go wrong in our times, is in their failure to realize that the New Testament model for churches is that they should be comprised of a plurality of pastors. In other words, each local church body should be governed by a group of pastors/elders, not one individual. This is clear from such texts as Acts 14:23 where we read, "And when they had appointed *elders* for them in every church…" Acts 20:17 also points to this plurality of elders/pastors, "From Miletus he sent to Ephesus and called to him the *elders* of the church." Writing to Timothy, Paul says, "Let the *elders* who rule well be considered worthy of double honor, especially those who labor in preaching and teaching" (1 Tim. 5:17). Many other passages refer to this plurality of elders/pastors in the local church (Titus 1:5, 1 Tim. 4:14, James 5:14, 1 Peter 5:1-3). Scripture makes it clear that the church is to be led by a group of elders/pastors.

---

70 Central ministry roles within the church according to the above passages consist of apostles, prophets, evangelists, pastor-teachers (or elders or overseers) and deacons. Many Christians today would see the function of apostles and prophets as roles restricted to the early New Testament church. There are compelling arguments that have been made that do not hold such restrictions. For clarity concerning this issue see Sam Storms, "Are Apostles For Today?" (November 6, 2006); available from www.enjoyinggodministries.com/article/are-apostles-for-today/; accessed 17 March 2010.

The Functions of Elders

So what is the function of a pastor? And why does the term "pastor" mean the same as the term "elder"? A pastor very simply is one who leads and shepherds God's people. A pastor is one who preaches and teaches the Word of God to the people of God. The fact that "elder" is just another word for pastor is clear from Scriptures such as 1 Tim. 5:17, which reads, "Let the elders who rule well be considered worthy of double honor, especially those who labor in preaching and teaching." If pastors are ones who govern the church and lead by preaching and teaching, it is clear that the word elder is just another term for the office of pastor. Paul addresses the elders in Ephesus, saying, "Pay careful attention to yourselves and to all the flock, in which the Holy Spirit has made you overseers, to care for the church of God, which he obtained with his own blood" (Acts 20:28). Peter exhorts the elders to "shepherd the flock of God" (1 Pet. 5:2a). What is clear in these passages is that elders are the ones who shepherd or pastor the church.

Sadly, this understanding of eldership is a foreign concept for many Christians. "When most Christians hear of church elders, they think of an official church board, lay officials, influential people within the local church, or advisors to the pastor. They think of elders as policymakers, financial officers, fund raisers, or administrators. They don't expect church elders to teach the Word or be involved pastorally in the lives of people....Such a view, however, not only lacks scriptural support but flatly contradicts the New Testament Scriptures. One doesn't need to read Greek or be professionally trained in theology to understand that the contemporary, church-board concept of eldership is irreconcilably at odds with the New Testament definition of eldership. According to the New Testament concept of eldership, elders lead the church, teach and preach the Word, protect the church from false teachers, exhort and admonish the saints in sound doctrine, visit the sick and pray, and judge doctrinal issues. In biblical terminology, elders shepherd, oversee, lead, and care for the local church."[71]

In summary, the functions of the elders/pastors involves leading and governing the local church (1 Tim. 5:17) by preaching and teaching God's Word (1 Tim. 3:2; 5:17), guarding against false teaching (Titus 1:9, Acts 20:28-31) and doing everything possible to care for and build up the body of Christ (Acts 20:28, Eph. 4:11-16).

The Qualifications of Elders

One of the major attacks on biblical truth in our day and age is in the area of biblical manhood and womanhood. In our culture, equality across genders equals the ability and even rightness of functioning in the same roles, regardless of gender distinctions. In other words, women can and should be able to do anything and everything that a man can do and men can and should be able to do anything and everything a woman can do. Yet according to biblical manhood and womanhood, men and women are created equal in the image of God, but perform distinct roles and functions that compliment each other. As Christ sacrificially leads the church, so the husband is to lead the wife; and as the church submits to Christ, so the wife is to submit to the husband (Eph. 5:22-33). Not only do men and women relate to each other differently in marriage but also within the church. "Let a woman learn quietly with all submission. I do not permit a woman to teach or to exercise authority over a man; rather, she is to remain quiet. For Adam was formed first, then Eve..." (1 Tim. 2:11-13).

What we see here in these verses is that by God's gracious and wise design, men and women have different roles in the church.

---

71 Alexander Strauch, *Biblical Eldership: An Urgent Call to Restore Biblical Church Leadership* (Littleton, CO: Lewis and Roth Publishers, 1995), 15-16.

Women play a deeply significant role in the life of the church, but they are not to have a teaching office that is over men within the church. Godly men are to lead the church. This difference in roles is not a changing cultural phenomenon that only applied to Timothy's day, but is rooted in God's perfect and unchanging design displayed at creation (v. 13). Thus, one of the qualifications of elders/pastors is being a man. Only men can be elders/pastors within the local church.

However, just being a man does not make one qualified to be an elder. Much more is needed to bear such a weighty task. Paul lists the necessary qualifications in 1 Timothy 3:1-7:

> "The saying is trustworthy: If anyone aspires to the office of overseer, he desires a noble task. Therefore an overseer must be above reproach, the husband of one wife, sober-minded, self-controlled, respectable, hospitable, able to teach, not a drunkard, not violent but gentle, not quarrelsome, not a lover of money. He must manage his own household well, with all dignity keeping his children submissive, for if someone does not know how to manage his own household, how will he care for God's church? He must not be a recent convert, or he may become puffed up with conceit and fall into the condemnation of the devil. Moreover, he must be well thought of by outsiders, so that he may not fall into disgrace, into a snare of the devil."

A willing desire, strong godly character, good leadership in the home, and teaching abilities are all required for one to be an elder of a church. To become an elder is to take on a weighty task with weighty responsibilities. An elder is one who must watch over souls and "who will have to give an account" (Heb. 13:17). Indeed, the one who "aspires to the office of overseer ...desires a noble task."

Deacons

Though elders have the noble task of overseeing and governing the life of the church, there is a need for others to take part in leadership. In 1 Timothy 3:8-13, we also see another office within the local church and the qualifications necessary to function in its role: the office of deacon. It seems clear that the seven men appointed to administrate and take care of the social needs within the church, as mentioned in Acts 6:1-6, refer to the early development of the office of deacon. "In general, the verses on deacons show that they had recognized offices to 'serve' the church in various ways. Acts 6:1-6 suggests that they had some administrative responsibilities, but were nevertheless subject to the authority of those who had rule over the entire church."[72] Deacons are not to lead and function with the same authority of elders. Under the elders' authority, deacons are to help provide oversight for the social needs of the church.

The Importance of Commitment to the Local Church

Individualism and consumerism have been two defining marks of our contemporary culture. Though we all long for community, the Western mind has been largely driven by an individual-centered way of thinking. To a large degree, our choices and behavior are governed by the assumption that life revolves around the individual. We live with the constant questions of, "How will this affect me? How will this please me?" Thus, our choices and way of living are isolated from community insight and community regard. That is why we see so many divorces. Instead of looking

---

72 Wayne Grudem, *Systematic Theology: An Introduction to Biblical Doctrine* (Grand Rapids, MI: Zondervan, 1994), 919-920.

out for the interests of the family as a whole, people look out for their own individual interests and happiness. This individualistic way of thinking leads to fickle and uncommitted relationships.

In turn, this individualistic outlook on life promotes a lifestyle of consumerism. Being governed first and foremost by the question, "how will this please me?" will lead to consumption of anything and everything that achieves this goal of self-gratification. With the countless options of food and entertainment in our society, one can pick, choose, consume, and move on to the next item as often as one likes. It is all about the satisfaction of the individual customer.

This individualism and consumerism has also taken root among Christians and has affected the way we approach church. It keeps us from being committed and deeply involved in the life of a local church community. As a whole, we have lost the meaning of the word "commitment" altogether and have become far removed from the reality of the New Testament teachings concerning the local church.

Church membership is a reality that has been lost in the church today. I do not just mean signing a card, but I refer to something much more. True church membership means being committed and deeply ingrained within the life of the church. It means submitting to the leaders and being held accountable for what you believe and how you live. It means recognizing the need for others to help you grow in the Christian life. It means being a contributor and not just a consumer. Just attending church on Sunday is not enough and does not reflect the sort of commitment to the church that the New Testament calls for.

Hebrews 13:17 states, "Obey your leaders and submit to them, for they are keeping watch over your souls, as those who will have to give an account." Pastors will have to give an account to God concerning those souls who were under their care. Yet will pastors have to give an account of those who did not make themselves accountable by joining and being committed to the church? Joining and being committed to a church is necessary because it brings about a level of accountability that one would not have without joining.

The Scriptures speak of church discipline as one necessary mark of a true church. Paul, speaking to the Corinthian church, instructs them on what to do about an unrepentant sexually immoral brother. "Let him who has done this be removed from among you.... you are to deliver this man to Satan for the destruction of the flesh, so that his spirit may be saved in the day of the Lord" (1 Cor. 5:2, 5). The local church is to enact discipline by excommunicating the wayward believer, in hopes that he will be restored.

Jesus also gives us instructions concerning church discipline, saying, "If your brother sins against you, go and tell him his fault, between you and him alone. If he listens to you, you have gained your brother. But if he does not listen, take one or two others along with you, that every charge may be established by the evidence of two or three witnesses. If he refuses to listen to them, tell it to the church. And if he refuses to listen even to the church, let him be to you as a Gentile and a tax collector" (Matt. 18:15-17). The almost total lack of proper church discipline in the church today is tragic. We have lost this important characteristic and have not realized its great importance to the health of the local body.

Church discipline is meant to be done for the good of wayward believers, yet if professed Christians do not become members of a church, they will not be able to be subject to this discipline, and thus will keep themselves free from life-giving accountability. The danger of this can be seen in the following example. A certain man has been a strong believer for a number of years and has been attending a particular church for a while. He begins to engage in a committed relationship with a non-believer and starts living in sexual immorality. If he were a member of the church, he would be disciplined and through that discipline possibly might be restored. Being committed to a local church is important because it brings an essential level of accountability to your life.

Not only does commitment to the local church bring healthy accountability but it also opens the door for much spiritual growth. We need the local church and leaders of the local church in order for us to grow into Christ-like maturity. "And he gave the apostles, the prophets, the evangelists, the pastors and teachers, to equip the saints for the work of ministry, for building up the body of Christ, until we attain to the unity of the faith and of knowledge of the Son of God, to mature manhood, to the measure of the stature of the fullness of Christ, so that we may no longer be children, tossed to and fro by the waves and carried about by every wind of doctrine, by human cunning, by craftiness in deceitful schemes. Rather, speaking the truth in love, we are to grow up in every way into him who is the head, into Christ, from whom the whole body, joined and held together by every joint with which it is equipped, when every part is working properly, makes the body grow so that it builds itself up in love" (Eph. 4:11-16). It is through the local church and our church leaders that we are empowered to grow into a strong and healthy body of believers. In fact, each person within the church is needed to help the growth of the church (1 Cor. 12:21-24).

Ultimately, "the church community is where we learn to love God and others; where we are strengthened and transformed by truth from the Word; where we're taught to pray, to worship, and to serve; where we can be most certain that we're investing our time and abilities for eternity; where we can grow in our roles as friends, sons and daughters, husbands and wives, fathers and mothers. The church is earth's single best place—God's specially *designed* place—to start over, to grow and to change for the glory of God."[73]

It is important and required to be committed to the local church, not just for the sake of our own spiritual growth, but also for the sake of contributing to the spiritual growth of others. As Christians, we are called to be contributors, not just consumers. All Christians have been given spiritual gifts by God that must be used for His glory. It is disobedience to God not to put your spiritual gifts to use in the context of the local church. Paul says, "Let us use them: if prophecy, in proportion to our faith; if service, in our serving; the one who teaches, in his teaching; the one who exhorts, in his exhortation; the one who contributes, in generosity; the one who leads, with zeal; the one who does acts of mercy, with cheerfulness" (Rom. 12:6-8).

We must realize that ministry is not just for the leaders of the church. "All Christians are called to ministry. Because we are followers of him who said he had come not to be served but to serve (Mark 10:45), it is inconceivable that we should spend our lives in any other way than ministry or service. But there is a wide diversity of gifts, callings and ministries, and we have to discover our gifts and help others to discover theirs."[74] There are many spiritual gifts listed in the New Testament (1 Cor. 12:1-11, Rom. 12:6-8, Eph. 4:11, 1 Pet. 4:9-11). What are your gifts, and how can you use them within your local church?

Exhortation: Stick Together as the Day Draws Near

As the Second Coming of Jesus approaches, we must be ready and prepared. That readiness and preparation will largely take

---

73 Joshua Harris, *Stop Dating the Church: Fall in Love with the Family of God* (Colorado Springs, CO: Multnomah Books, 2004), 21.
74 Stott, *The Living Church*, 74-75.

place within the context of the local church. As the Day fast approaches, we must stick together in order to endure and persevere till the end. There can be no lone wolf Christians, especially in the dark days that we are living in and the even darker ones that are on the horizon. We desperately need each other. We desperately need the local church to endure the days of increased deception, temptation and persecution that are ahead. Are you committed to a local church that is faithfully preaching the Word of God? Are you committed to a local church that is bearing the characteristics of a healthy church? May God have mercy on us and revive our churches and our commitment to them.

CHAPTER 9
Be Watchful

Baseball was one of my favorite sports as a child. Before I stepped up to bat, my grandpa would always say to me, "Keep your eye on the ball." When it came to baseball, this seemed to be the only advice he ever gave me. Due to the frequency and repetition of this single charge, I knew it must have been something really important to consider. This charge: "Keep your eye on the ball," indeed was very important, and even has greater significance as we consider what it means to be ready for the return of Christ.

For us to be ready for the return of Christ, we must keep our eye on the ball of our culture and world. We must be watchful concerning the world we live in. For us to persevere until the end and make contact with our returning King, we must keep our eye on what's going on in the world and what's going on in our own hearts. We must be watchful!

When we look upon our world, we realize that we are living in troubling times.

"It is good for Christians to take some time to look at the trouble, for all around us are darkening skies and gathering clouds. As we engage this culture and look at it honestly, we must sense that something has happened— and is even now happening—in our culture. These major shifts will change everything we know about ministry in terms of the challenge before us and will draw out the reality of who the church is in the midst of a gathering conflict. Clouds are darkening.

"We are no longer seeing the first signs of cultural trouble, but rather the indicators of advanced decay. The reality is that people now do not even know what they have lost, much less that they themselves are lost.

"...There is a sense, I think, in this culture that we are waiting for a signal for something to tell us which way we are going to go. Something is happening and about to happen. The landscape is changing, the skies are darkening—and this is something we know with a spiritual perception, a spiritual sense, a spiritual urgency. Something is happening that we as believers in the Lord Jesus Christ should see and understand."[75]

If you observe our world and culture with a thinking mind and spiritual eyes, you will notice the changes and the darkness that surrounds us. But what is it exactly that is happening?

"Consider what is even now happening in our midst. We are witnessing the dawn of a post-Christian age in our own times, in our own nation, in our own world, and among our own people...Something is happening to the worldview, the mentality, and the consciousness of this age. If we listen closely, we can hear something like the closing of a steel door—a solemn, cataclysmic slamming of a door. We have been watching the postmodern mind in its development, and it is now well developed. Not

75 R. Albert Mohler, Jr., *The Disappearance of God: Dangerous Beliefs in the New Spiritual Openness* (Colorado Springs, CO: Multnomah Books, 2009), 157-159.

only do we see the themes of postmodernity taking hold of the larger culture, but we understand the challenge this pattern of thinking poses to Christian truth and Christian truth-telling. Tolerance is perverted into radical secularism that is anything but tolerant. There is little openness to truth, and growing hostility to truth claims. Indeed, the postmodern mind has a fanatical, if selective, dedication to moral relativism, and an understanding that truth has no objective or absolute basis whatsoever."[76]

How are we going to respond to these changing times? How are you going to respond to the dark times we are living in? We must "be sober-minded, we are told. Gird up the loins of your thinking. Be ready, be alert, be watchful. Be a watchman on the wall. Have your eyes open. Be ready for action. This is our calling as Christians, even as the darkness gathers. We are to be a community of the open-eyed, the intellectually alert, the brokenhearted, and the resolutely hopeful."[77]

Be Watchful

This charge to be watchful, I believe, is the essence and main point of Matthew 24-25:13. After describing all those things that must take place before Jesus returns, Jesus continues His discourse in verses 32-51 saying:

> "From the fig tree learn its lesson: as soon as its branch becomes tender and puts out its leaves, you know that summer is near. So also, when you see all these things, you know that he is near, at the very gates. Truly, I say to you, this generation will not pass away until all these

---

76 Ibid, 163, 165-166.
77 Ibid, 174.

things take place. Heaven and earth will pass away, but my words will not pass away.

"But concerning that day and hour no one knows, not even the angels of heaven, nor the Son, but the Father only. For as were the days of Noah, so will be the coming of the Son of Man. For as in those days before the flood they were eating and drinking, marrying and giving in marriage, until the day when Noah entered the ark, and they were unaware until the flood came and swept them all away, so will be the coming of the Son of Man. Then two men will be in the field; one will be taken and one left. Two women will be grinding at the mill; one will be taken and one left. Therefore, stay awake, for you do not know on what day your Lord is coming. But know this, that if the master of the house had known in what part of the night the thief was coming, he would have stayed awake and would not have let his house be broken into. Therefore you also must be ready, for the Son of Man is coming at an hour you do not expect.

"Who then is the faithful and wise servant, whom his master has set over his household, to give them their food at the proper time? Blessed is that servant whom his master will find so doing when he comes. Truly, I say to you, he will set him over all his possessions. But if that wicked servant says to himself, 'My master is delayed,' and begins to beat his fellow servants and eats and drinks with drunkards, the master of that servant will come on a day when he does not expect him and at an hour he does not know and will cut him in pieces and put him with the hypocrites. In that place there will be weeping and gnashing of teeth."

In Matthew 25:1-13 Jesus says, "Then the kingdom of heaven will be like ten virgins who took their lamps and went to meet the bridegroom. Five of them were foolish, and five were wise. For when the foolish took their lamps, they took no oil with them, but the wise took flasks of oil with their lamps. As the bridegroom was delayed, they all became drowsy and slept. But at midnight there was a cry, 'Here is the bridegroom! Come out to meet him.' Then all those virgins rose and trimmed their lamps. And the foolish said to the wise, 'Give us some of your oil, for our lamps are going out.' But the wise answered, saying, 'Since there will not be enough for us and for you, go rather to the dealers and buy for yourselves.' And while they were going to buy, the bridegroom came, and those who were ready went in with him to the marriage feast, and the door was shut. Afterward the other virgins came also, saying, 'Lord, lord, open to us.' But he answered, 'Truly, I say to you, I do not know you.' Watch therefore, for you know neither the day nor the hour."

Starting with Matthew 24:32-33, Jesus says, "From the fig tree learn its lesson: as soon as its branch becomes tender and puts out its leaves, you know that summer is near. So also, when you see all these things, you know that he is near, at the very gates." Jesus is teaching us something very important about His Second Coming. He is telling us, "When you look at a fig tree and observe certain characteristics of the fig tree, you can tell what season it is. In the same way, when the final generation observes the signs I have just mentioned concerning my return (verses 4-28), they will know that it is the season of my return. They will know that I am near, at the very gates." In essence, Jesus is saying, "Be watchful, because when you see these particular signs taking place, you will know that I am near. If you are watching, and you see these signs take place, you will know the general season of my return."

So how do we reconcile the statement, "you will know that I am near," with the statement, "concerning that day and hour no one knows?" I believe the difference between these two statements is that on one hand it is possible to have a general knowledge of the season of Christ's return, and on the other hand it is impossible to know the exact time. Those watching and waiting for Christ's return can know the general season and nearness of His return, and yet no one knows the exact timing of His return.

And yet the sad thing is that many people abuse the statement "concerning that day and hour no one knows" and take it out of its proper context. Many quote this verse and in essence say, "No one knows the day or the hour, so we don't need to be preoccupied with all this end times stuff." Yet within the context of this statement, Jesus is telling us to be watchful and pay serious regard to the things concerning His return. It is true that we are not to set dates, and it is obvious that many people have gone to crazy extremes concerning end times teachings, but just because there have been abuses does not mean we can fall to the other extreme and neglect the clear instructions of Jesus concerning watchfulness.

Jesus warns us that we do not want to be like all the people in Noah's day, who just went about life as usual, caught up in the world's affairs, and were suddenly, to their surprise, swept away in judgment (vs. 37-39). It will be the same way for many people when Christ returns. To warn us Jesus says, "Therefore, stay awake, for you do not know on what day your Lord is coming. But know this, that if the master of the house had known in what part of the night the thief was coming, he would have stayed awake and would not have let his house be broken into. Therefore, you also must be ready, for the Son of Man is coming at an hour you do not expect" (vs. 42-44).

What I believe Jesus is driving home to us is this: You don't know the exact time of my return. That is why you need to stay awake and be watchful. Keep your eyes on me and on eternity. Do not be swallowed up in the affairs of this life. If you stay awake and are watchful concerning the signs that will precede my return, you will be ready and unsurprised when I come. You will not be shocked or taken off guard. Therefore, stay awake.

At this point, some of you may be thinking, "I see what you are saying, but doesn't Scripture say He will come suddenly like a thief? Won't we all be surprised?" Jesus will come like a thief to the world, but not to true Christians. "Now concerning the times and seasons, brothers, you have no need to have anything written to you. For you yourselves are fully aware that the day of the Lord will come like a thief in the night. While people are saying, 'There is peace and security,' then sudden destruction will come upon them as labor pains come upon a pregnant woman, and they will not escape. *But you are not in darkness, brothers, for that day to surprise you like a thief*" (1 Thess. 5:1-4, emphasis mine). For true Christians, Jesus' coming will not be a surprise. We will not be thrown off and unprepared.

It is clear from our passage in Matthew that the ones who are shocked and unprepared are those of the world and those who are professing Christians yet not truly born again. In Matthew 24:37-39, we see that the unbelieving world will be shocked and surprised at Jesus' Second Coming. Speaking of those who are a part of the visible church and yet were not truly born again, Jesus says that "the master of that servant will come on a day when he does not expect him and at an hour he does not know" (v. 50). To the professing Christians at Sardis, Jesus said, "If you will not wake up, I will come like a thief, and you will not know at what hour I will come against you" (Rev. 3:3). To fake Christians who are asleep, He will come like a thief. He will not come like a thief to those true Christians who are awake and watching.

In the parable of the ten virgins in Matthew 25:1-13, we see Jesus giving an illustration to drive home the seriousness of being watchful concerning His return. There will be many within the visible church like these five foolish virgins who were unprepared to meet the Bridegroom. Yet those who truly know Christ will have their lamps burning and will be ready to meet their beloved Bridegroom. Those who are awake and watching will truly be blessed. "Stay dressed for action and keep your lamps burning, and be like men who are waiting for their master to come home from the wedding feast, so that they may open the door to him at once when he comes and knocks. Blessed are those servants whom the master finds awake when he comes. Truly, I say to you, he will dress himself for service and have them recline at table, and he will come and serve them. If he comes in the second watch, or in the third, and finds them awake, blessed are those servants!" (Luke 12:35-38).

What to Watch For

Ok, so we know that as Christians we are to be awake and watchful concerning Christ's return, but what exactly are we to watch for? Jesus' instructions to be watchful in Matthew 24 and 25 are in context of the signs concerning His return, just previously mentioned earlier in chapter 24. Though these signs have been mentioned throughout the book, we will give a brief recap here in no particular chronological order:

Sign 1 The Ingathering of Israel

In Matthew 24:3 Jesus' disciples ask the question, "What will be the sign of your coming and of the close of the age?" From that point on, Jesus proceeds to mention those things that will take place before He returns. Before we briefly summarize those signs mentioned in chapter 24, we notice one sign that is mentioned at the end of chapter 23. Speaking to Jerusalem, which represents the Jewish people as a whole, He says, "For I tell you, you will not see me again, until you say, 'Blessed is he who comes in the name of the Lord'" (v. 39). Here Jesus is saying that He is about to die, rise and go to the Father. The Israelites will not see Him again until they embrace Him as the Messiah. Before Jesus comes back, there will be a great ingathering of the Jews back into the covenant. "All Israel will be saved" (Rom 11:26), before Jesus returns.

Sign 2 Global Catastrophes

In chapter 24, we see that one of the signs of His near return will be global catastrophes. "And you will hear of wars and rumors of wars. See that you are not alarmed, for this must take place, but the end is not yet. For nation will rise against nation, and kingdom against kingdom, and there will be famines and earthquakes in various places. All these are but the beginning of the birth pains" (vs. 6-8). Though these realities have happened throughout the course of history, there will an increase of war among the nations and an increase in natural and supernatural disasters (see Revelation chapters 6, 8-9 and 16).

Sign 3 Increase of Persecution

"Then they will deliver you up to tribulation and put you to death, and you will be hated by all nations for my name's sake" (Matt. 24:9). Though persecution has always been a reality in the church, there will be an increase of persecution before Christ returns (Rev. 6:9-11; 13:5-7; 17:5-6).

Sign 4 A Great Falling Away

"And then many will fall away and betray one another and hate one another" (Matt. 24:10). Many within the visible church will turn away from Christ, betray the church, and be filled with hatred toward the people of God. There will be a massive falling away.

SIGN 5 INCREASE OF DECEPTION

"And many false prophets will arise and lead many astray... For false christs and false prophets will arise and perform great signs and wonders, so as to lead astray, if possible, even the elect" (Matt. 24:11, 24). There will a mighty increase of deception and false teaching that will cover the earth. There will be many false christs and false prophets. There will also arise one known as the antichrist or man of lawlessness or the beast (Matt. 24:15, 2 Thess. 2:3-12, Rev. 13), who together with the false prophet (Rev. 13:11-17) will deceive the nations.

SIGN 6 INCREASE OF UNGODLINESS

"And because lawlessness will be increased, the love of many will grow cold" (Matt. 24:12). Before Christ returns, there will be a massive increase of ungodliness and wickedness in the earth. The great Babylonian world system will pollute the earth with increased sexual immorality, idolatry and greed (Rev. 17-18).

SIGN 7 THE FULFILLMENT OF THE GREAT COMMISSION

"And this gospel of the kingdom will be proclaimed throughout the whole world as a testimony to all nations, and then the end will come" (Matt. 24:14). The good news of God's kingdom of grace revealed in Jesus will spread to all tribes and peoples. God will save a people and establish His kingdom among every people group of the world before Jesus returns. God's people, by the power of the Holy Spirit, will finish the great commission before the King consummates His kingdom.

SIGN 8 A GREAT OUTPOURING OF THE HOLY SPIRIT

Though not mentioned in Matthew 24, Acts 2 reveals a great outpouring of the Holy Spirit as predicted by Joel, partially fulfilled at Pentecost, which will yet have a future and complete fulfillment before the return of Christ. "'And in the last days it shall be, God declares, that I will pour out my Spirit on all flesh, and your sons and daughters shall prophecy, and your young men shall see visions, and your old men shall dream dreams; even on my male servants and female servants in those days I will pour out my Spirit, and they shall prophesy. And I will show wonders in the heavens above and signs on the earth below, blood, and fire, and vapor of smoke; the sun shall be turned to darkness and the moon to blood, before the day of the Lord comes, the great and magnificent day. And it shall come to pass that everyone who calls upon the name of the Lord shall be saved'" (Acts 2:17-21).

The mighty and supernatural power of God will be poured out upon the church and a harvest of salvation will come to the lost before the day of the Lord.

SIGN 9 GREAT SIGNS AND WONDERS

With this great outpouring of the Holy Spirit will come spectacular signs and wonders. "And I will show wonders in the heavens above and signs on the earth below, blood, and fire, and vapor of smoke; the sun shall be turned to darkness and the moon to blood, before the day of the Lord comes, the great and magnificent day" (Acts 2:19-20). "Immediately after the tribulation of those days the sun will be darkened, and the moon will not give its light, and the stars will fall from heaven, and the powers of the heavens will be shaken. Then will appear in heaven the sign of the Son of Man..." (Matt. 24:29-30). Not only will God bring about mighty signs and wonders upon the earth and in the heavens, but false christs along with the false prophet and the anti-christ, will display false signs and wonders (Matt. 24:24, 2 Thess. 2:9, Rev. 13:11-15). Those who love the truth will be able to discern true signs from false signs (2 Thess. 2:9-12).

The Heart of Watchfulness

There are two more things I want to point out from Matthew 24 concerning watchfulness. It is not enough as a Christian just to be watching and aware of these signs that must take place before Christ returns. For us to be ready for His return, Jesus requires two things of us that are mentioned in Matthew 24. We must be living useful and holy lives unto the Lord.

In Matthew 24:45-46, we see that we are to be living useful lives unto the Lord. "Who then is the faithful and wise servant, whom his master has set over his household to give them their food at the proper time? Blessed is that servant whom his master will find so doing when he comes." We are to be faithful and wise servants of our Lord Jesus who take part in bringing nourishment and edification to the family of God. We are to use our time, money, gifts, and energy well by helping to build up the body of Christ and by bringing the good news of Jesus to this lost world. To be ready for Jesus' Second Coming, we must be useful servants of our Master.

We also see that at the heart of true watchfulness is living a life of holiness. "But if that wicked servant says to himself, 'My master is delayed,' and begins to beat his fellow servants and eats and drinks with drunkards, the master of that servant will come on a day when he does not expect him and at an hour he does not know and will cut him in pieces and put him with the hypocrites. In that place there will be weeping and gnashing of teeth" (Matthew 24:48-51). The useful servant is a holy servant. Those unholy servants, who do not pay regard to the Master's coming, will be thrown into eternal punishment. Those who have truly put their faith in Jesus will be living a holy life in anticipation for

His return. Love for God and love for people will be the characteristics of their lives.

The heart of true watchfulness has to do with watching one's
own heart and guarding against worldliness. "But watch yourselves
lest your hearts be weighed down with dissipation and drunkenness and cares of this life, and that day come upon you suddenly
like a trap" (Luke 21:34). Jesus has told us, "Watch and pray that
you may not enter into temptation" (Matt. 26:41). Because our
hearts are corrupt and prone to evil, we are vulnerable to the lies
and attacks of the evil one. Therefore we are commanded: "be sober-minded; be watchful. Your adversary the devil prowls around
like a roaring lion, seeking someone to devour. Resist him, firm
in your faith…" (1 Pet. 5:8-9).

In essence, to live useful and holy lives unto the Lord in anticipation for His return, we need to take heed to the Scriptural
exhortations that are summed up in the chapter titles of this book.
To be ready for Christ's return, we must deeply desire and long for
His return. We must love the truth of His holy and perfect Word.
We must love the gospel truth, that in grace beyond compare,
Christ died in the place of us wretched sinners and rose again
in victory to bring us forgiveness and eternal life through faith
in Him alone. We must pursue Christ-likeness and use our time
well. We must endure suffering as good soldiers of Jesus Christ.
We must take part in finishing the great commission. We must
pray and fast for His coming. We must be committed to a gospel-
centered local church. We must be watchful. By God's grace and
for His glory, we must heed these exhortations. Are you pursuing
these realities in your life?

Closing Vision and Exhortation

What it comes down to is this: I want you to be ready to
behold the glory of King Jesus. I want your eyes and your heart

to be ready to take in the beautiful sight of His appearing. I want you even now to behold this vision by faith until your faith turns to sight when He comes again. Hear the words of Jesus with great anticipation:

> "Immediately after the tribulation of those days the sun will be darkened, and the moon will not give its light, and the stars will fall from heaven, and the powers of the heavens will be shaken. Then will appear in heaven the sign of the Son of Man, and then all tribes of the earth will mourn, and they will see the Son of Man coming on the clouds with power and great glory. And he will send out his angels with a loud trumpet call, and they will gather his elect from the four winds, from one end of heaven to the other" (Matt. 24:29-31).

Hear the words of the prophet Daniel with great excitement:

> "I saw in the night visions, and behold, with the clouds of heaven there came one like a son of man, and he came to the Ancient of Days and was presented before him. And to him was given dominion and glory and a kingdom, that all peoples, nations, and languages should serve him; his dominion is an everlasting dominion, which shall not pass away, and his kingdom one that shall not be destroyed" (Daniel 7:13-14).

Our glorious King Jesus is coming again with power and great glory. He is coming back in all of His splendor and majesty. He is coming back with all power and authority. He is coming back to rule and reign forever as the supreme King over all the earth. He will resurrect all of God's chosen children from every people, nation, and language, and He will gather them into His arms of everlasting love. We will joyfully worship and serve Him and the Father forever. Oh, what a glorious day it shall be when He returns to set up His perfect and indestructible kingdom!

As one has written, on that day God's people "shall go in with the Bridegroom to the marriage. They shall be forever in the company of Christ, and go out no more. Faith shall then be swallowed up in sight. Hope shall become certainty. Knowledge shall at length be perfect. Prayer shall be turned into praise. Desires shall receive their full accomplishment. Hunger and thirst after conformity to Christ's image shall at length be satisfied. The thought of parting shall not spoil the pleasure of meeting. The company of saints shall be enjoyed without hurry and distraction. The family of Abraham shall no more feel temptations; nor the family of Job, afflictions; nor the family of David, household bereavements; nor the family of Paul, thorns in the flesh; nor the family of Lazarus, poverty and sores. Every tear shall be wiped away in that day. It is the time when the Lord shall say, 'I make all things new.'

"Oh, reader, if God's children find joy and peace in believing even now, what tongue shall tell their feelings when they behold the King in His beauty! If the report of the land that is far off has been sweet to them in the wilderness, what pen shall describe their happiness, when they see it with their own eyes? If it has cheered them now and then to meet two or three like-minded in this evil world, how their hearts will burn within them when they see a multitude that no man can number, the least defects of each purged away, and not one false brother in the list! If the narrow way has been a way of pleasantness to the scattered few who travelled it with their poor frail bodies, how precious shall their rest seem in that day of gathering together, when they shall have a glorious body like their Lord's! Then shall we understand the meaning of the text, 'In Thy presence is fullness of joy, and at Thy right hand are pleasures forevermore' (Psalm 16:11)."[78]

May your heart take comfort and be filled with joy as you look forward to the time when intimacy with our triune God will be completely consummated (Rev. 19:6-9, 21:3), when our bodies will be resurrected and glorified (1 Cor. 15:12-23, 50-57; Phil. 3:20-21; 1 Thess. 4:13-18), when the kingdom of the Lord will come in fullness (Rev. 2:25-27, 20:1-6) and when the earth will be renewed and restored to the way God planned (Rom. 8:20-22, 2 Pet. 3:10-13, Rev. 21-22:5).

May this amazing hope transform you here and now.

May your life be filled with passion for the glory of God as you anticipate the day the fullness of His glory shall be revealed. By God's grace, I charge you to watch and get ready.

"Let us watch for our Lord Jesus Christ's sake. Let us live as if His glory was concerned in our behavior. Let us live as if every slip and fall was a reflection on the honor of our King. Let us live as if every allowed sin was one more thorn in His head, one more nail in His feet, one more spear in His side. Oh, let us exercise a godly jealousy over thoughts, words and actions, over motives,

---

78 J.C. Ryle, *Are You Ready For The End of Time?* (Scotland, UK: Christian Focus Publications, 2001), 32-33.

manners, and walk. Never, never let us fear being too strict. Never, never let us think we can watch too much. Leigh Richmond's dying words were very solemn. Few believers were ever more useful in their day and generation. Of few can it be said so truly, that he 'being dead yet speaketh.' But what did he say to one who stood by, while he lay dying?

'BROTHER, BROTHER, WE ARE NONE OF US MORE THAN HALF AWAKE!'"[79]

Let this not be said of anyone of us. Let us be ones who have loved His appearing (2 Tim. 4:8) and who will be found fully awake and ready when He comes again. Are you ready for Jesus to come back?

"I ask you, 'Are you ready?' Remember the words of the Lord Jesus, 'They that were ready went in with the bridegroom to the marriage': they that were ready and none else. Now here, in the sight of God, I ask each and every reader, is this your case? Are you ready?

"I do not ask whether you are a churchman, and make a profession of religion. I do not ask whether you attend an evangelical ministry, and like evangelical people, and can talk of evangelical subjects, and read evangelical tracts and bookseller, and may be easily attained. I want to search your heart more thoroughly, and probe your conscience more deeply. I want to know whether you have been born again, and whether you have got the Holy Ghost dwelling in your soul. I want to know whether you have any oil in your vessel while you carry

79 Ibid, 39.

the lamp of profession, and whether you are ready to meet the Bridegroom, ready for Christ's return to the earth. I want to know, if the Lord should come this week, whether you could lift up your head with joy, and say, 'This is our God; we have waited for Him; let us be glad, and rejoice in His salvation.' These things I want to know, and this is what I mean when I say, 'Are you ready?'"[80]

Oh, God, revive your church and wake us up to the near return of our Lord Jesus Christ!

---

80   Ibid, 34-35.

FOR MORE ABOUT THE AUTHOR
AND HIS WRITINGS, PLEASE VISIT:

www.wakeupchurch.net